W9-AQA-188

Discovering What Works for Struggling Readers

Journeys of Exploration

With Primary-Grade Students

Bev Wirt

Carolyn Domaleski Bryan

Kathleen Davies Wesley

Peoria Unified School District

Glendale, Arizona, USA

LIBRARY
FRANKLIN PIERCE COLLEGE
RINDGE, NH 03461

INTERNATIONAL
Reading
Association

800 Barksdale Road, PO Box 8139
Newark, Delaware 19714-8139, USA
www.reading.org

IRA BOARD OF DIRECTORS

MaryEllen Vogt, California State University Long Beach, Long Beach, California, President • Richard Allington, University of Florida, Gainesville, Florida, President-elect • Timothy Shanahan, University of Illinois at Chicago, Chicago, Illinois, Vice President • Cathy Collins Block, Texas Christian University, Fort Worth, Texas • James Flood, San Diego State University, San Diego, California • Victoria J. Risko, Peabody College of Vanderbilt University, Nashville, Tennessee • Charline J. Barnes, Adelphi University, Garden City, New York • Rita M. Bean, University of Pittsburgh, Pittsburgh, Pennsylvania • Carrice L. Cummins, Louisiana Tech University, Ruston, Louisiana • David Hernandez, III, Washington DC Public Schools, Washington, DC • Susan Davis Lenski, Portland State University, Portland, Oregon • Jill Lewis, New Jersey City University, Jersey City, New Jersey • Alan E. Farstrup, Executive Director

The International Reading Association attempts, through its publications, to provide a forum for a wide spectrum of opinions on reading. This policy permits divergent viewpoints without implying the endorsement of the Association.

Editorial Director   Matthew W. Baker
Managing Editor   Shannon T. Fortner
Permissions Editor   Janet S. Parrack
Acquisitions and Communications Coordinator   Corinne M. Mooney
Associate Editor   Charlene M. Nichols
Books and Inventory Assistant   Rebecca A. Zell
Assistant Permissions Editor   Tyanna L. Collins
Production Department Manager   Iona Muscella
Supervisor, Electronic Publishing   Anette Schütz
Senior Electronic Publishing Specialist   R. Lynn Harrison
Proofreader   Elizabeth C. Hunt

Project Editor   Charlene M. Nichols

Cover   Design, Linda Steere; Photo, Image Productions

Copyright 2005 by the International Reading Association, Inc.

All rights reserved. No part of this publication may be reproduced or transmitted in any form or by any means, electronic or mechanical, including photocopy, or any information storage and retrieval system, without permission from the publisher.

Web addresses in this book were correct as of the publication date but may have become inactive or otherwise modified since that time. If you notice a deactivated or changed Web address, please e-mail books@reading.org with the words "Website Update" in the subject line. In your message, specify the Web link, the book title, and the page number on which the link appears.

Library of Congress Cataloging-in-Publication Data
Wirt, Bev, 1950-
  Discovering what works for struggling readers : journeys of exploration with primary-grade students / Bev Wirt, Carolyn Domaleski Bryan, Kathleen Davies Wesley.
     p. cm.
  Includes bibliographical references and index.
  ISBN 0-87207-008-5
  1. Reading—Remedial teaching—United States—Case studies. 2. Reading (Primary)—United States—Case studies. 3. Individualized instruction—United States—Case studies. 4. Group reading—United States—Case studies. I. Bryan, Carolyn Domaleski, 1949- II. Wesley, Kathleen Davies, 1952- III. Title.
  LB1525.76.W57 2004
  372.43—dc22

2004020920

To our young readers for their inspiration and to our families
and friends for their encouragement and support on this journey
—we are grateful.

Contents

Chapter 5

Note From the Series Editor

It is a pleasure to introduce readers to Bev Wirt, Carolyn Domaleski Bryan, and Kathleen Davies Wesley and the primary-grade students whom they write about in *Discovering What Works for Struggling Readers: Journeys of Exploration With Primary-Grade Students*.

In this book, we are provided the opportunity to look closely at how primary-level teachers—Bev, Carolyn, and Kathleen—and their students worked together to foster literacy learning. The teachers describe several "points of action" that became crucial to the reading instruction they designed in the context of their district's reading intervention program—Literacy Enrichment for Accelerated Progress (LEAP). Five teaching principles form these points of action: (1) meaningful conversations, (2) choice, (3) pertinent instruction, (4) consistent support, and (5) purpose. I am pleased that this researched-based report of several teachers' work was selected by a respected panel of literacy experts to be published in the Kids InSight (KI) series; I believe that the book makes an outstanding contribution to the field of elementary-level students' literacy development. I also would like to acknowledge the work of Sharon Arthur Moore, who was integral in the creation and implementation of the LEAP program in the authors' school district.

The KI series provides practical information for K–12 teachers and brings to the fore the voices of and stories about children and adolescents as the basis for instructional decisions. Books in the series are designed to encourage educators to address the challenge of meeting the literacy needs of all students as individuals and learners in and out of our classrooms, while recognizing that there are no easy answers or quick fixes to achieving this goal. Sociocultural perspectives of how students learn are the foundation of each KI book, and authors address learners' emotional, affective, and cognitive development. Strategies and actions embraced by teachers described in KI books include the following:

- dialoguing with other professionals;
- reading research findings in literacy and education;
- inquiring into teaching and learning processes;
- observing, talking with, and listening to students;
- documenting successful practices; and
- reflecting on literacy events using writing and analysis.

Authors of these books allow us to see into classrooms or view students' lives outside school to learn about the thoughts and dreams of young people, as well as the goals and planning processes of teachers. Finally, we are privy to how events actually unfold during formal and informal lessons—the successful and the less-than-successful moments—through the use of transcripts and interview comments woven throughout KI books.

As we read *Discovering What Works for Struggling Readers*, Bev, Carolyn, and Kathleen show us how to keep students *in sight* when they describe the initial assessments they use to understand the students' strengths and the literacy skills and strategies that they struggle with. The teachers also seek to develop familiar lesson structures and patterns of interaction to provide students with the predictability they need to achieve in school. The book also does a nice job of showing how the points of action allowed three students—Allison, Joshua, and Brianna—to improve in their reading abilities. Finally, the teachers all rely on strong family support for literacy development. These educators outline what they learn from caregivers that helps them meet students' needs within school, how they build relationships with families, and how they create special experiences that help parents support literacy learning in and out of school (e.g., Family Literacy Night).

Bev, Carolyn, Kathleen, and their students also help us glean insights as we examine what teachers and students do together during literacy lessons that results in improved reading behaviors. For example, we are privy to specific examples of one-on-one lessons where teachers work individually with Allison, Joshua, and Brianna on word-study activities, exploration activities, writing lessons, and selecting the right texts for a child at the right time. The three teachers focus on helping students see reading as purposeful and they attend to motivation as a key element in all of their lesson planning. Several struggles are outlined that help readers see that it is critical to understand the students' motivations for participating in a particular activity (or not) and why they find a task purposeful (or not). The goal for all lessons is to help students realize success and to feel a sense of self-efficacy about the tasks they undertake.

Throughout *Discovering What Works for Struggling Readers*, Bev, Carolyn, Kathleen, and their colleagues help readers grapple with teaching and learning issues by urging us to write responses to questions posed, gather data from our classrooms, reflect on what we see, and generate new possibilities for what could be. They also challenge us to see what can be accomplished when skillful teachers work individually with students, over an extended period of time, to provided specific or "pertinent" instruction that moves a child forward. By the time you finish reading these three in-depth case studies, you will feel as though you had participated in these classrooms and interacted with Allison, Joshua, and Brianna over an extended period of time. You also will see the power of knowledgeable, dedicated literacy teachers and the difference they can make in the lives of individual students.

Deborah R. Dillon

Series Editor

University of Minnesota, Twin Cities

Minneapolis, Minnesota, USA

Kids InSight Review Board

JoBeth Allen
University of Georgia
Athens, Georgia, USA

Deanna Birdyshaw
CIERA
Ann Arbor, Michigan, USA

Fenice B. Boyd
University of Buffalo (SUNY)
Buffalo, New York, USA

Faye Brownlie
Vancouver, British Columbia,
  Canada

Richard C. Culyer
Coker College
Hartsville, South Carolina, USA

H. Gay Fawcett
Nordonia Hill City Schools
Stow, Ohio, USA

Robert Fecho
University of Georgia
Athens, Georgia, USA

Lee Galda
University of Minnesota
Minneapolis, Minnesota, USA

William A. Henk
Marquette University
Milwaukee, Wisconsin, USA

Gay Ivey
James Madison University
Harrisonburg, Virginia, USA

Sharon Arthur Moore
Glendale, Arizona, USA

David G. O'Brien
University of Minnesota
Minneapolis, Minnesota, USA

Lisa Cross Stanzi
David C. Barrow Elementary
Athens, Georgia, USA

Melvin L. Thursby
Prairie Middle School
Cedar Rapids, Iowa, USA

Jan Turbill
University of Wollongong
Wollongong, New South Wales,
    Australia

Angela Ward
University of Saskatchewan
Saskatoon, Saskatchewan, Canada

Deborah A. Wooten
University of Tennessee
Knoxville, Tennessee, USA

Josephine P. Young
Arizona State University
Tempe, Arizona, USA

Chapter 1

Working With Struggling Readers: How Our Journey Began

"Is it my turn to read with you today, Mrs. Wirt? Please, please, please! Did you find any more snake books?"

"Yes, Allison. It's your turn."

Mrs. Wirt smiles and hands Allison a copy of Snake's Dinner *(Saltis, 1999).*

"Does it have a real snake in it? Let's read it!"

Joshua's dance resembles that of a spirited football player who has just made his first touchdown. "Mrs. Wesley, I did it! I did it!" he exclaims. He has just finished reading My Accident *(Giles, 1996). This is the first time Joshua chose and used strategies to decode every word in a book. And he did it all by himself!*

"Teeny Tiny Tina.../l/.../l/..."—Brianna pauses for a moment and then resumes reading Teeny Tiny Tina *(Butler, 1989)—"lives in a teeny tiny house!"*

"Wow!" exclaims Mrs. Bryan. "How did you figure out lives?"

"I did what we talked about yesterday," Brianna answers. "I skipped that word and read some more. Then, when I looked at it again, I knew it! I'm gonna do that all the time now when I get stuck."

As teachers, we know the excitement of sharing those life-changing moments with our students when they comprehend the previously unknown. Allison, Joshua, and Brianna led us—Bev Wirt, Carolyn Bryan, and Kathleen Wesley—on yearlong journeys of exploration into the complexities of learning to read. The journey began for us when we, three reading teachers from the same school district, worked together in a professional writing class. As a project for this course, each of us analyzed and reflected on her documentation of a year of interactions and lessons with a particular student. The one-to-one teaching format of our district's reading intervention program—Literacy Enrichment for Accelerated Progress (LEAP)—gave us the opportunity to focus on individual students in this way. We hoped to find common elements that led to student success to use to strengthen our own instruction and to share with other teachers.

In this chapter, we begin by explaining the framework of the reading program we used. Then, we discuss the five common teaching principles we discovered. Finally, we introduce each teacher and the students she worked with during the year of study.

The Context of Our Work and What We Discovered

The LEAP Program

The students' work that we documented and analyzed was completed within the context of the LEAP program. The goal of LEAP is to accelerate the progress of first- and second-grade struggling readers by supporting and extending good classroom teaching. (See Box 1.1 for a list of materials used to design LEAP.) This support is offered by combining individual and small-group reading instruction in a separate classroom. Five groups of four students each attend 45-minute daily sessions in the LEAP classroom. A Literacy Intervention Teacher (LIT) who holds a state reading endorsement and a minimum of three years' teaching experience leads the program in the classroom. A Reading Instructional Assistant (RIA)—a high school graduate who has participated in a district-designed training program—assists the LIT.

On a given day, three students work with the RIA as the fourth student works with the LIT. The next day, a different student from the group meets with the LIT. This rotation continues four days per week so that each student has one individual lesson and three small-group lessons during a regular week. On the fifth day, this rotation can continue or become a focus lesson involving all four students.

Box 1.1
A Few of the Texts Used to Design the LEAP Program

Cunningham, P.M., & Allington, R.L. (1999). *Classrooms that work: They can all read and write.* New York: Longman.

Moore, S.A., & Moore, D.W. (1991). Knowing when and what to teach. *The Reading Teacher, 44,* 502–503.

Pikulski, J.J. (1994). Preventing reading failure: A review of five effective programs. *The Reading Teacher, 48,* 30–39.

Slavin, R.E., Karweit, N.L., & Wasik, B.A. (1992/1993). Preventing early school failure: What works? *Educational Leadership, 50*(4), 10–18.

Taylor, B.M., Short, R.A., Frye, B.J., & Shearer, B.A. (1992). Classroom teachers prevent reading failure among low-achieving first-grade students. *The Reading Teacher, 45,* 592–597.

During the 45-minute individual lesson with the LIT, a student begins by participating in a teacher-directed word study and then rereads a familiar story as the LIT takes a running record for oral reading analysis. Next, the student writes a sentence in a personal draft book. In response to the sentence, the LIT often provides a spontaneous lesson. After listening to the LIT introduce a new book, the student reads it and reacts to a teaching point specified by the LIT. Finally, the student selects books to take home and rereads several independent-level books.

The RIA's lesson may begin with self-selected reading. Students also write in their draft books, reread familiar stories, select books to take home, and participate in a word-study lesson using either a word wall or a making-words format in which a student uses a specific set of letter cards to make words. A fifth activity focuses on comprehension. This part of the lesson alternates between extending and supporting the classroom reading program or retelling and dramatizing stories.

During focus lessons, the LIT selects a quality piece of children's literature. The LIT chooses activities to apply comprehension strategies or to practice specific composition skills. For example, after reading *The Little Red Hen* (Barton, 1993), students might focus on sequence by reenacting the story. Next, students could place pictures of story events in the correct order. Finally, the students could compose sentences for each picture.

The Points of Action

As the three of us shared our analyses of the students' work in the LEAP program, we came to the conclusion that five teaching principles were not only evident but also key to the gains each child experienced in all three of our summaries: (1) meaningful conversation, (2) choice, (3) pertinent instruction, (4) consistent support, and (5) purpose. We named these five principles "points of action" and believe they are crucial in all reading instruction, if not all instruction.

One point of action is not effective without the other four points. Meaningful conversation stimulates and develops thought patterns. It helps the teacher know the students and lays the foundation of trust. Choice is motivating and engages the students. There are many opportunities daily to empower students with ownership using choice. Pertinent instruction allows the students to move ahead at their own personal pace for success. The teacher offers each student only what is necessary for his or her own literacy growth. Consistent support offers students a constant, clear view of the important aspects of learning to read. Therefore, it is important for people with compatible reading philosophies to teach and support the child. Purpose is the students' guide to learning. It provides the students with direction and can be the motivation to read. Each of these points of action played an important role in the successes of our students.

These five points of action involve more than skill and strategy instruction. They focus all teaching on the needs of the child. Preservice teachers, beginning teachers, and even experienced teachers will find that the points of action provide a powerful framework for meeting each student's needs. As you read, you will see how the points of action allowed Allison, Joshua, and Brianna to experience reading improvement and success.

*Reflection Point 1.1*_____

Journals are important tools we use to record our observations, thoughts, and conclusions about our work with our students. The reflection points in this book ask you to reflect, analyze, and draw conclusions. You will make connections to your classroom and share ideas with colleagues. Recording this information in a journal will allow you to notice patterns of behavior and thought. This can be a guide to your future teaching decisions.

Recall a shining moment when a student response to a lesson exceeded your expectations. How did the student feel? How did you feel? What factors contributed to this success?

Meaningful Conversation. So often students are taught *to* and talked *at*. These approaches do not stimulate the development of any skills except, perhaps, listening. In meaningful conversations, one person's ideas stimulate another person's ideas and vice versa. Both people's thoughts continue to build into meaningful connections and concepts. Meaningful conversation acknowledges where students are developmentally and who they are. It also helps to build and expand the students' framework for learning and teaches them to link the new with the old. Reading skills—including making comparisons or contrasts, noticing cause and effect, sequencing, and determining and recalling important details—also are developed through these exchanges.

Ellin Oliver Keene, one of the authors of *Mosaic of Thought: Teaching Comprehension in a Reader's Workshop* (1997), shares many examples of meaningful conversations. One example details the experiences of a second-grade child, Anne, who was determined to read *The Secret Garden* (Burnett, 1911), even though the teacher feared the book clearly exceeded Anne's reading abilities. The teacher helped Anne begin the book and then introduced her to a fifth-grade student, Kristin, who had already read and enjoyed the book. During the girls' regular meetings, Kristin guided Anne to a deeper understanding of the text by posing questions about the book to help Anne find her own interpretations. Keene's work illustrates the effectiveness of using meaningful conversation to expand comprehension instruction.

Patricia Cunningham and Richard Allington (1999) describe a teacher who successfully integrates meaningful conversation into his or her daily routine as follows:

> The teacher tries to talk to each child during the morning center time and spends a few extra minutes with the children she has identified as being most needy. For her children whose English is limited either because English is not their first language or because they have had few real conversations with adults, she makes sure to engage them in some conversation about what they are doing at the center. (p. 210)

Teachers who engage in meaningful conversation with their students cannot help but better understand the students' thought processes, strengths, and limitations. Meaningful conversation leads each student and the teacher to greater understanding of each other.

In chapter 3, Kathleen shares her experiences with Joshua. His limited experiences with meaningful conversation were reflected in pre-reading dialogues conducted to activate his prior knowledge. Until Joshua had built a foundation of trust and a framework for expressing and connecting his past experiences, Kathleen was unsure of his understandings. Kathleen, taking time to build this relationship, develop a sense of trust, and involve him in opportunities to express himself, allowed Joshua to gain self-confidence and blossom. He became aware that he, too, had valuable ideas to contribute and could be successful.

Reflection Point 1.2

Carolyn uses an analogy to describe meaningful conversation: "It is like a flower in bloom. It opens minds, makes connections, and pollinates the seeds of new ideas." Create your own analogy to describe meaningful conversation. Share this analogy with several colleagues.

Choice. Students assume ownership of their learning when given the power of choice. Linda Gambrell (1996) supports this notion when she says, "Motivation and reading development are fostered when children are immersed in a book-rich environment, engaged in interactions with others about books, and given the responsibility for making decisions about what, when, and how they read" (p. 14).

Regie Routman (2003) goes even further when she says that teachers disenfranchise students by making all the choices for them. Conversely, by allowing students to make decisions and choices, teachers show respect for students and give value to students' thinking.

In Richard Allington's (2002) description of the practices of effective teachers, he specifies that the tasks teachers assign are meaningful and challenging, integrate several content areas, and offer student choice.

We found that nothing motivated our students to read as much as the opportunity to choose their own books. They could choose topics they found interesting or wondered about. They could choose fiction or nonfiction texts based on what they felt like reading that day. They could reread favorites or try something new.

We incorporated choice in our lessons in other ways, too. During writing activities, students often determined what they wished to write about a particular book they had read and, at times, they chose not to write about a book at all. We gave students the opportunity to choose from two or three activities planned to meet particular instructional needs. For example, to meet the need for practicing specific high-frequency words, students could choose to form words with pipe cleaners, magnetic letters, or markers. Some opportunities for choices were as simple as selecting the color of a marker to use. We found that the power of choice resulted in students engaging more fully in their lessons.

Choice was a powerful motivator for Brianna. At times, she was attracted to books that Carolyn felt were too difficult. Brianna may have been attracted to the cover or the title of a given book, but whatever the attraction, she would work harder on getting through that book because it was her own choice. She would take the book home to work on it with her family and come back excitedly sharing her favorite parts with her classroom teacher and her LEAP group, never once mentioning any difficulties. Brianna also focused more on sentence-writing activities when she was able to choose her own materials. The color of the sentence strip paper, the color of the marker, and the book she wanted to write about all were important decisions for her.

Reflection Point 1.3

List classroom situations in which students are involved in decision making to achieve specific goals. Remember, choices exist in many aspects of a lesson, including selecting writing topics, choosing a book or an activity, or choosing between using markers or crayons. What are some additional situations in which you could offer your students choices?

Pertinent Instruction. Our one-to-one lesson format allowed us to see more easily which strategies each student was using and which he or she had not yet fully developed or even discovered. It helped us determine in which skills a student was strong and in which he or she needed scaffolding. We agree with Allington's (2001) belief that "teachers should be decision-makers, using their practical, personal, and theoretical knowledge to inform their reading instruction" (p. 124). Consequently, our instruction was pertinent because it served to bridge gaps between the known and the unknown. No student took too great a leap or an unnecessary one. All students learned what they needed, when they needed it. This type of pure teaching guarantees success.

The reality of a classroom filled with students of varying levels may make implementation of this point of action seem overwhelming. Grouping students to most efficiently support their needs for reaching their potential has been a dilemma in organized education. Tracking, advanced placement classes, self-contained classrooms, and red bird–blue bird groupings all have been designed to effect this. Currently, teachers can make pertinent instruction a real possibility through frameworks such as guided reading groups and flexible groupings.

Marie Clay (1988) states the importance of pertinent instruction in *Reading Recovery: A Guidebook for Teachers in Training*:

> Here I want to add a critical note. Educators have individualised the rate at which they introduce children to programmes, but I do not believe we have paid sufficient attention to individualising the tasks and instruction that we provide during that period. It is not only that these children are moving at different rates; some of them need more help with

some aspects of the task than others. We need to think more about children taking different paths to similar outcomes. (p. 3)

The "path" a student needs to take must be determined by observing the
student's reading behaviors. Instruction is pertinent only when founded
on formal or informal assessments of each student's specific needs. A
thorough analysis of a combination of teacher observations, conversations with the student, evidence of student performance, and formal
assessments provides the framework for instruction.

Teachers need to understand that each child's path is different.
Sharon Taberski's words in *On Solid Ground: Strategies for Teaching
Reading K–3* (2000) reflect our own findings that each child has his or
her own specific needs at any given time:

I believe in being "systematic," but in wise ways—in ways that make
sense to children. Children don't need strategies and skills presented in
specific order, but in relation to their needs as they arise in the course
of reading and writing. (p. 95)

Our goal was and is to know our students, their needs, and their motivations and to provide opportunities for pertinent instruction to help
them continue in their literary growth.

Allison struggled with the concept of monitoring her own voice-to-
print correspondence. Making this an actual objective was a way of
providing pertinent instruction for her. Cut-up sentences of her own
composition offered one way to point out words. Using a card as a reading guide focused her reading and supported her development of this
understanding. Locating specific words in text helped her notice beginning and ending sounds. These were pertinent activities because they
directly supported Allison's specific need at that time.

Reflection Point 1.4

Recall a recent day in your classroom. How many ways—in one
day—did you differentiate instruction to make it pertinent to
student needs? What would you do differently?

To take advantage of more opportunities to address individual student needs, use Figure 1 to focus on each of your students and provide for special needs at least once during each week. This activity will help increase your awareness of the uniqueness of each student in your class.

Consistent Support. The reading teacher is certainly not the only influence on students' literacy development. The classroom teachers and care providers also play major roles in the attitudes of our students and their learning attempts. When all these people work together, students have a clear picture of their goal and are not confused about how to approach it. Strong connections developed through good communication among the classroom, the home, and the LEAP team were essential to the success of our students.

Irene Fountas and Gay Su Pinnell (1996) speak to this issue in their book *Guided Reading: Good First Teaching for All Children*:

> Literacy is constructed by each child individually but this does not mean he does it alone. Literacy learning is facilitated by interactions with other, more knowledgeable readers. The role of caregivers and teachers is critical in children's opportunities to become literate. Adults demonstrate reading and writing and support children as they begin to participate in literacy events. Sometimes, they explain important concepts about written language; often, they encourage children by noticing evidence of effective processing. Parents and teachers demonstrate, explain, and support. They help children attend efficiently and meaningfully to visual information in print and to use that information in a dynamic way in connection with their knowledge about language. (p. 18)

Consistent support requires that all adults working with a child agree on a reading philosophy. This philosophy might include the following principles:

- Children need to read at their own appropriate levels.
- Children need to read frequently.
- Children need to converse meaningfully about their reading.
- Children need everyone to acknowledge their growing independence.
- Children need positive reading models.

Whatever philosophy guides the instruction, consistency is the key.

Figure 1
Student Needs Focus Chart

Student	Need	Pertinent Instruction
Mary	Fluency	Reread favorite book to three different buddies this week.
John	Can't sit still to read	Walk around the room and read all the words to a partner (Read the Room).

Celebrating each small step of growth as well as the big steps is part of Carolyn's philosophy. Brianna's classroom teacher and family shared the same philosophy. For example, after analyzing the word *vegetable* using Elkonin sound boxes (i.e., a row of boxes, each containing one sound), Brianna discovered that she could not only read the word but also spell it from memory. She triumphantly shared her new skill with her classroom teacher, her classmates, and her family. They all joined Carolyn in marveling at Brianna's wonderful accomplishment. Consistent support made this a special moment and fueled Brianna's confidence and enthusiasm for learning.

Reflection Point 1.5

What is your philosophy about reading? Interview a parent, an administrator, and another teacher at your school. Ask them to share their beliefs about reading. Compare their beliefs to your own reading philosophy. If they differ, what steps would build a more unified philosophy for your school?

Purpose. Jerry Johns and Susan Davis Lenski (1997) point out that emergent readers may not even realize the different reasons for reading. These authors encourage teachers to help children understand that people read for particular purposes. Cunningham and Allington (1999) write,

> Children who are successful at becoming literate view reading and writing as authentic activities from which they get information and pleasure, and by which they communicate with others. They know what reading and writing are really for and want to be successful at it. The literacy-rich classroom communicates the importance of real reading and writing activities by engaging children in a variety of print activities and not relegating reading and writing to a brief period. (p. 21)

Teacher modeling can inspire students to value and claim these purposes. Teachers must emphasize the practical nature of reading. Older students would readily recognize the importance of being able to read a drivers' manual, while younger students love reading environmental print such as names of their favorite restaurants. An effective way to motivate struggling readers is for teachers to continually share their own purposes for reading (Johns, 2001).

Routman (2003) agrees:

> As teachers we need to examine what we do as a reader and make our thinking and practices visible to our students. Our students admire us and seek to emulate us. When we make our reading lives explicit to our students, their reading lives expand in many directions. (p. 25)

Although Allison showed continual growth in Bev's LEAP group, when her friend graduated from the LEAP program, Allison fully embraced a new purpose: She wanted to graduate, too. Her whole attitude changed. This purpose motivated Allison to accelerate her attempts to progress to grade-level reading. Bev's prompts to improve Allison's fluency now had more value to this student. Allison had been aware of the ultimate purpose of LEAP; however, when she witnessed another student advancing out of the program, she realized this was something she could do as well.

A child's purpose may be a surprise for a teacher. Allison tried harder because she wanted to exit LEAP. Brianna worked for attention and to please the teacher. Realizing that he could be successful through his own efforts motivated Joshua. Other children read voraciously because of special interests they have in specific topics. Teachers need to be aware of their students' goals and interests so they can use the power of the child's personal sense of purpose.

Reflection Point 1.6

Two special posters are always part of Kathleen's classroom décor. These posters visually represent her purposes for teaching children to read. Make your own posters to portray to your students the value of and purposes for reading. Use photographs, pictures from magazines, computer clip art, or whatever else illustrates your intent. Consider having your students contribute original art for this project.

We applied the points of action in our work with students while using the components of the LEAP program. However, we believe that using these points of action will add to the success of any reading program.

The Teacher and Student Pairs

Now that you have a basic understanding of the LEAP program and the five points of action, we will introduce ourselves and the students with whom we worked. Although the names of the students are pseudonyms, they represent actual children.

Bev and Allison

Bev's book-filled classroom at Marshall Ranch Elementary School, Glendale, Arizona, USA, says to students, "You won't leave here without being an eager and capable reader!" Bev has been an educator for 21 years in primary-grade classrooms in rural Missouri and Kansas as well as in a private school, an inner-city school, and suburban schools in the Phoenix area. Bev has been a reading specialist for six years and earned a master's degree in elementary education from Arizona State University. As an adjunct instructor for Grand Canyon University, she also learns from working with teachers pursuing their master's degrees.

Marshall Ranch School is a K–8 school surrounded by an enclave of upper middle class homes. The school also enrolls students from lower to middle income apartment complexes. Of the 956 students enrolled during the year of this experience, 44.6% are Caucasian, 38.8% are Hispanic, and 16.6% are designated as Other. Only 18.8% of these students are eligible for free or reduced-cost lunches.

Allison is a first-grade student who achieved the goal of the LEAP program—she exited before the end of the year. Allison is the third of four girls in her family. Her mother does not work outside the home and seems involved in helping Allison learn to read. Allison is a sociable child, and she lavishes time not spent with her friends on her pet snake.

Bev Wirt: I chose Allison because she comes from a school that does not teach phonics in kindergarten and because she is so unwilling to attempt new tasks for fear of being wrong. She does seem to have a strong oral vocabulary, however, and I feel her family will really work with us.

Kathleen and Joshua

You only have to spend a few minutes with Kathleen to know that she is always seeking new ways to reach her students. Kathleen has been an educator for 19 years. She earned her master's degree in reading education from Rhode Island College. Having worked with teachers and children in Arizona, Rhode Island, and Washington, DC, Kathleen has been a special education teacher, lead teacher, and Title I reading specialist. She also has been an adjunct faculty member for a graduate program in special education. Kathleen has been a Literacy Intervention teacher for eight years.

Set in the southernmost section of the district, Sun Valley Elementary School is a Title I school surrounded by a combination of new housing, trailer parks, and cotton fields. The demographics of the school are constantly changing. Of the 1,400 students, 55.1% are Caucasian, 33.3% are Hispanic, and 11.6% are described as Other. Free and reduced-cost lunch students are 37.1% of the population.

Joshua is a first grader who is the middle child in a family of three boys. He is more outgoing with his brothers than with his peers. Both of his parents work outside the home, and a grandmother helps with some of the child care. Having worked with his older brother, Kathleen is aware of the necessity to provide all support Joshua needs at school. Although Joshua's mother sought outside reading assistance for her sons, she did not always follow through on reading with and to her children.

During his time in the LEAP program, Joshua struggled with more than a reading problem. Although not significant enough to qualify for special services, Joshua's expressive language was delayed. Together, Kathleen and Joshua worked to increase his use of oral language, to help him realize he can use reading strategies independently, and to develop his comprehension skills. He made great progress but was not quite ready to exit the LEAP program at the end of first grade.

Kathleen Wesley: I wrote about Joshua because he is so quiet. I was concerned about his language development.

I taught his brother, but they are not alike. Joshua has more alphabetic skills but is less verbal so it's hard to tell how much he understands.

Carolyn and Brianna

Carolyn is perpetually searching for ways to make a positive difference in the lives of her students. She has been an educator for 32 years, having taught in Michigan, Colorado, and Arizona. As a classroom teacher, she taught grades 3 through 9. She also has been a Title I reading teacher, a reading resource teacher for 10 years, and a Literacy Intervention teacher for 7 years. A graduate of Michigan State University, she worked on her master's degree in reading education at the University of Northern Colorado.

Canyon Elementary School is the smallest school in the district, with a population of 488 students, including the students in the special education center housed on the campus. Caucasians make up 84% of the school population, Hispanics make up 11%, and 5% are described as Other. The school neighborhood includes many acre and half-acre horse properties as well as middle class to lower middle class homes. There are no multiple-family dwellings, and most homes are 20 to 25 years old. The free lunch population is 21.6%.

Brianna is a chatty, outgoing, savvy little girl. She and her older brother live with an aunt and uncle. Overcoming a serious illness in early childhood, dealing with an unstable home life early on, and attending several different schools before entering second grade all influenced Brianna's attitudes toward and expectations of school and herself.

Although Brianna made great strides during the LEAP program, she did not reach grade-level competence. Key factors in Carolyn's work with Brianna included developing confidence, finding effective motivation, and providing pertinent instruction for this child whose skills were far below grade-level expectations.

Carolyn Bryan: I wrote about Brianna because she had such a rough beginning. Now that she is in second grade and her life situation has stabilized somewhat, I'm hoping that the extra one-to-one might really help her get on track with her reading.

Why We Wrote This Book

We believe that successful reading experiences in the primary grades are crucial to future success in school—and life. As educators, we are always looking for ideas to improve reading instruction. It was in this quest that we found the great value of the five points of action. If you apply these points of action in your teaching of reading, you will find that your students will be more confident, motivated, and involved, and your teaching decisions will be focused and relevant.

Organization of This Book

Chapters 2 through 4 recount the individual struggles and successes of the young learners—Allison, Joshua, and Brianna—as they become readers. Each chapter is organized in a different format. In chapter 2, Bev presents her information chronologically to provide the reader with a clear, sequential look at a school year. In chapter 3, Kathleen reports Joshua's progress by developmental book levels to demonstrate that understandings build on earlier understandings through a definite progression. In chapter 4, Carolyn organizes Brianna's growth in word work, reading, and writing by quarterly assessment periods to show the relation between instruction and assessment.

Chapter 5 presents additional ideas teachers can use to bring the points of action into their own classrooms.

Join us on this yearlong journey with Allison, Joshua, and Brianna. We challenge you, however, to be more than a simple observer. As you read their stories, think of your own students. Let this book lead you to your own discoveries. All students have their own unique stories from which teachers can learn. Be alert to their messages; they are enlightening.

Chapter 2

A Year With Allison: Finding a Purpose

Bev's LEAP group is sitting around a table enjoying a celebratory treat of hot wings. Allison's mom and younger sister have joined the group for Allison's graduation celebration.

Mrs. Germain:	*How did you become such a good reader?*
Allison:	*By practicing every day and by thinking while I am reading!*
Robert:	*What was your favorite book?*
Allison:	*All the books about snakes!*

[The students react with a chorus of groans.]

Mrs. Germain:	*We will miss all your snake stories.*
Beth:	*Not me! I think snakes are disgusting! But I do like hot wings! When I graduate from LEAP, I want hot wings, too.*
Allison's mom:	*We are so proud of Allison. She reads all the time now. She reads to her little sister every day. I hope each of you graduates. It takes a lot of practice to be a good reader!*
Bev Wirt:	*Mrs. Germain and I love to celebrate graduations. Keep working and we may have another graduation party soon! Allison, please give your letter to your Mom telling her what a great job you have done, and here is a special book to enjoy and as a memory of LEAP. Now it's time for us to get back to our job of reading.*

The celebration of a student's exit from our LEAP program is our goal, yet each one is an emotion-filled event for my RIA, Barb Germain, and me, Bev Wirt, the LIT. We work together as the LEAP team at our site, Marshall Ranch Elementary School. This graduation was the culmination of many efforts and connections with Allison. Her success makes us confident of her future as a reader, yet we are very attached to her. Allison will continue to check out books from the LEAP classroom collection of leveled books for daily practice, and we will communicate with her classroom teacher frequently. With Allison's graduation, a new student, excited to become a "LEAP kid," enters our program. We welcome this new challenge. Each child participating in LEAP has a unique story; this is Allison's.

Meeting the Students

During the initial week of school, Barb and I visit each of the four first-grade classrooms. We introduce ourselves and share our purpose of helping students become great readers. Then, I share the entertaining and interactive book *Froggy Goes to School* (London, 1996) and introduce a large stuffed frog. After listing the students' suggestions of names for the frog, we tell students that some of them will get to come and visit our room and vote on a name for the green mascot. This is only the first of many opportunities for students to make choices and take ownership in the LEAP classroom and program.

Children are selected for assessments using input from their kindergarten teachers, their current teachers, or their parents. Allison first visited our LEAP classroom during the second week of the school year because her kindergarten teacher had expressed concerns for Allison's success in reading. Once in the LEAP classroom, Allison and a classmate spent a few moments perusing the room and checking out the tiny African Dwarf frogs in the aquarium.

We designed our classroom environment to be welcoming and unique as well as functional. Our half-sized classroom is filled with books; colorful, comfortable seating; and our collection of frogs—stained glass, wood carvings, books, pillows, stuffed animals, wind socks, ceramics, wall hangings, photographs, and student drawings. The frog theme has definitely caught the students' attention because they describe us as "the frog teachers" on our campus. The girls each cast a vote to select a name for the stuffed frog mascot, who ultimately became known as Frogger.

Initial Assessments

Allison met with Mrs. Germain to complete the Ohio Word Test to evaluate her sight-word vocabulary, the Writing Vocabulary Observation to gain insight into her letter–sound connections, and the Letter Identification assessment to determine her knowledge of the letters of the alphabet. Meanwhile, I worked with another student completing the Dictation Task to appraise her use of letter sounds and her understanding of writing conventions. I also used Stahl and Murray's Phoneme Awareness Assessment to evaluate her ability to blend and segment words, the Predictable Language Text Retelling Analysis to assess listening and comprehension, and a Consonant–Vowel–Consonant (CVC) Word List assessment to gather more information about her use of letter–sound knowledge and blending. Halfway through this session, the girls traded places and completed the tasks. These assessments provided a base for selecting students to participate in LEAP and for planning pertinent instruction (see Table 1 for Allison's initial assessment scores [September]).

Reflection Point 2.1

List the assessments you give to your students. Compare your list with your colleagues' lists or with those used in the LEAP program. Do these assessments identify patterns of strengths and limitations? Is this enough information or too much? How do you use this information?

Table 1
Allison's Assessment Summary

Date	Dictation Task	Letter Identification	Ohio Word Test	Phoneme Awareness	Writing Vocabulary	Oral Reading Analysis
September						
Raw Score	18/37	42/54	0/20	30/35	5	
Percentage	49%	78%	0%	86%		—
Stanine	5	4	1	—	2	—
November						
Raw Score	36/37	54/54	10/20		34	Level 11
Percentage	79%	100%	50%	—		79%
Stanine	9	9	7	—	6	—
January						
Raw Score	34/37	54/54	18/20		44	
Percentage	92%	100%	90%	—		98%
Stanine	8	9	9	—	7	—

Selecting the Participants

Our LEAP program accepts only 20 students at a time from the first-grade classes. Because I wanted to have all the information possible to make these important selections, I again met with each first-grade teacher. We discussed each child's assessment scores and classroom listening skills. I have found classroom listening skills to be an important indicator of reading success and one I cannot judge from my own assessments. Ms. Peters and I selected five participants from her class and sent the permission forms home for the students' parents to sign. Allison's assessment results placed her as the 3rd most struggling student in her classroom and the 11th most struggling student in her grade level, so she was invited into the LEAP program. One of the five students was assigned to a group with students from another first-grade classroom because each group can have only four students. The other four—Beth, Robert, Laura, and Allison—formed their own group.

Exploration Sessions

As we waited for parents to return permission forms, Mrs. Germain and I designed exploration sessions. The points of action are evident in our planning: We selected activities that would involve the students in meaningful conversations to learn more about our students and to develop a bond with them. We planned pertinent instruction to meet the needs of this group of students; we knew the students in Allison's group needed to practice letter names and sounds, so we planned to play several alphabet games. Because the students also were unsure of the concepts of word, letter, and sentence, we included activities to involve them in experiences with these concepts. The activities were designed to allow the students to explore the classroom materials and areas that had been designed to accomplish our purpose—helping our students become successful readers. Students would choose books to take home for practice each day, so we planned to model book selection. Finally, we planned activities to introduce important procedures necessary to offering consistent support, such as using draft books, take-home folders, and book boxes.

The initial assessments provided us with much information about Allison's current knowledge. Our assessments revealed that Allison could name 42 of 54 upper- and lowercase letters and pronounce sounds for 14 letters. The other members of her group had similar knowledge, so our first session offered pertinent instruction on letter identification. During this session, the four students were actively involved in several activities with letters. The enthusiastic participants played several short games of Alphabet Bingo. Next, each child used a pointer to indicate the letters on a chart as we sang the *ABC Song* to a variety of familiar tunes including *Row, Row, Row Your Boat; Mary Had a Little Lamb; Hot Cross Buns; Do You Know the Muffin Man?* and *Jack and Jill.* The children's favorite activity was a circle game of tossing a beach ball with alphabet letters printed on it. As the children caught the ball, they named the letters their hands touched. The students were quick to spot a classmate moving his hands to known letters and enjoyed tricking us by looking directly at a classmate but tossing the ball to one of us to catch us off guard. The small group offered more opportunity for meaningful conversation than the larger classroom group. We used this opportunity to become familiar with one another and to begin teaching our students to read using the points of action.

In the Dictation Task, Allison had correctly written most initial consonant sounds and several final sounds. However, the vowel sounds she included were confused, and she also ran her words together. Using a poem about names, which we printed on a large chart, Barb and I tried to connect the knowledge the students already had mastered to concepts of spacing and final word sounds. As we read this poem, we used a pointer to emphasize spaces between words and the words' final sounds. Next, we showed each child a card with his or her name printed on it. The consonants were black and the vowels were red. The color contrast made the vowels more obvious to the students. For example, Laura exclaimed to Allison, "Oh, look! We both have *a*'s in our names!" Robert and Beth retaliated with, "We both have *e*'s!" We use the students' names to model how to segment sounds, an important element of phonemic awareness. Allison was pleased to have the most sounds in her name.

Reflection Point 2.2_____

We found that using student names in classroom activities was highly motivational and allowed us to offer pertinent instruction. What are some other ways you can help children identify personally with tasks? Share your ideas with other teachers and create a reference list.

LEAP Practices

As previously mentioned, during exploration sessions we introduced students to the unique aspects of the LEAP program. These aspects include using draft books, selecting books, taking home "green pockets," and using book boxes.

Draft Books

We described draft books to our students as special, treasured, individual journals. Each student was instructed to record ideas, compliments, events, facts, and anything of importance in his or her book. During the exploration sessions, Mrs. Germain modeled composing and writing a sentence to emphasize directionality, word space, and letter size. The first sentence she used was "A cat sat on a mat." This supported the current classroom instruction, which was emphasizing the short sound for /a/. Allison and her group members all decided to write the modeled sentence in their draft books during the first few sessions.

Book Selection

Mrs. Germain and I compiled a special collection of books to use to introduce the book selection. We wanted this collection to include familiar stories, nursery rhymes, finger plays, books with illustrations corresponding directly to text, and book titles currently used in the classrooms. We chose books from this collection and modeled the thinking processes our students might use to select books to take home. For example, Mrs. Germain picked several books with dogs pictured on the cover and told the students, "I love to read books about dogs. I have a very special dog at home. She even looks a lot like the dog in this book." I selected a book and commented, "This book has a lot of words. I think I'll wait and read this later." We continued this discussion using additional books and then encouraged the students to do the same as they selected books.

Green Pockets and Book Boxes

Our students were excited about another unique aspect—"green pockets" to take home each day. Green pockets are zippered vinyl and nylon containers containing a spiral notebook for communication between LEAP personnel and parents, and several books to read at home. We also included other items such as paper "take-home books," word wheels or slides, and flashcards of high-frequency words for practice with parents. Students returned the green pockets to a plastic crate outside our classroom door each morning as they arrived at school. We then filled the pockets with new books and notes to parents and returned them to each student at the conclusion of each group's session. The information shared back and forth helped us all offer consistent support for the children.

To encourage our students to save the paper books we would be sending home frequently, Mrs. Germain and I gave each student a plastic shoe box, or book box. Students were pleased to use materials such as stickers, puffy paint, and trim to personalize their boxes. We explained the purpose of these special creations in a note to parents and suggested the boxes be kept in a special place in their homes.

By introducing students to the elements of LEAP, we gave them the opportunity to practice procedures and get to know us and the other members of the group. We believe these experiences help students feel secure and successful in our classroom. Mrs. Germain and I were eager to develop our connection to the parents and families of our students, too.

Families: Essential Support

Parent involvement is an important component of the LEAP program because the consistent support from home helps students experience success. We keep parents involved with special notebooks, a Family Literacy Night, and parent–teacher conferences. See Box 2.1 for additional resources on parent involvement.

Notebooks

The notebooks we send home in the green pockets provide a connection among parents, Mrs. Germain, and me. I also invite the classroom teachers to review these notebooks at any time to be aware of our communications. When we first began the LEAP program, we simply sent the notebooks and books home with the students each night. During our Parent Information Meeting, we reminded parents of the compact or agreement they had signed indicating that they would read each day with their children. Some of the students told us they rarely or never read the books at home. Others reported that their parents "listened" to them read while watching TV, cooking dinner, or driving.

Allison, however, received much support at home. Her parents were committed to daily reading practice and faithfully indicated practice by

---

Box 2.1
Resources on Parent Involvement

Allington, R.L. (Ed.). (1998). *Teaching struggling readers: Articles from* The Reading Teacher. Newark, DE: International Reading Association.

Allington, R.L. (2000). *What really matters for struggling readers: Designing research-based programs.* Boston: Allyn & Bacon.

Cullinan, B.E. (2000). *Read to me: Raising kids who love to read.* New York: Scholastic.

Kehlbeck, R. (2002). *I can do that with my kid? Family activities to encourage reading, writing, communication and positive self-esteem in children!* Dallas, TX: All My Heart Press.

Morningstar, J.W. (1999). Home response journals: Parents as informed contributors in the understanding of their child's literacy development. *The Reading Teacher, 52,* 690–697.

Neuman, S.B., Caperelli, B.J., & Kee, C. (1998). Literacy learning, a family matter. *The Reading Teacher, 52,* 244–252.

Zimmerman, S., & Hutchins, C. (2003). *7 keys to comprehension: How to help your kids read it and get it!* New York: Three Rivers Press.

---

initialing or signing the notebook. Allison's mother often shared observations of Allison' progress in her written comments. This consistent support was a powerful influence in Allison's growth as a reader.

Family Literacy Night

We held a Family Literacy Night in September so parents, students, their siblings, and Mrs. Germain and I could share a positive and informative literacy experience. Children participated in several frog-themed literature activities, including listening to a story, making paper bag puppets, creating bookmarks, and illustrating paper books, in the LEAP classroom with adult volunteers.

Meanwhile, in the nearby media center, Mrs. Germain and I involved the parents in some of the activities we had used with the children such as the making-words activity their children had done with Mrs. Germain that day. We had duplicated a section of our word wall on a bulletin board so parents could experience several favorite word wall games. I used *Read to Your Bunny* (Wells, 1997) to model appropriate before, during, and after reading questions. We also showed parents a sample draft book. Mrs. Germain relayed the purposes of the independent writing and reminded parents that these entries were unedited. I shared the purposes for writing during individual lessons and explained the cut-up sentence activity. Parents discussed ideas to incorporate daily reading with their children into their busy schedules. Several parents shared their experiences with older children who had been in LEAP. At the end of the evening, I responded to a few questions from parents.

A local book distributor donated a book for each family to take home. We also provided each family with a folder filled with bookmarks, a pencil, a booklet about the LEAP program, several pamphlets promoting family reading, and a set of letters for making-words activities. We were pleased with 90% attendance and the opportunity to connect with the parents of our students in a productive format. This was a true example of school, community, and family dedication to literacy development.

Parent–Teacher Conferences

Parent–teacher conferences also offer opportunities for parents, classroom teachers, and LITs to connect to offer consistent support for students. During the first year of LEAP, the first-grade teachers and I decided to meet with parents together to demonstrate the teamwork involved for their children. I met with the teachers before conferences to select one focus area for each child. Then, I started each conference with a brief report of the student's strengths, the focus the teacher and I had selected, and a suggestion to assist the parents in best helping their child. Rather than staying for the remainder of the meeting, I then excused myself and left.

The classroom teachers found this conference format very helpful and effective. It provided a place to start their discussions with parents and a tactful way of indicating, "Your child needs much support to become a successful reader. These are things we are doing; we hope you will be involved, too."

Allison's mother attended a parent–teacher conference in October. She shared her pride in Allison's gains in reading and reported that the whole family enjoyed a reading time each evening. Allison sometimes read her books to her younger sister. Her older sisters talked about the books they were reading. I reported that Allison's strength was using all the letter sounds and that our focus was to encourage her to use meaning to decode challenging words as she read. I suggested that giving Allison time to solve words would be beneficial and reminding her to think about a word that would make sense would be helpful. Ms. Peters, Allison's mother, and Mrs. Germain and I were offering Allison consistent support for growth—an important element of our points of action.

Our efforts to involve parents in our reading program were rewarding and frustrating. Many parents were pleased to have opportunities to learn how best to help their children. They also appreciated the opportunity to meet the parents of their child's classmates. We observed new friendships among the parents of our students develop because of our meetings, and although a few parents remained unresponsive, the successes we experienced made our efforts worthwhile. We have seen students benefit from the consistent support developed by these connections, and in this case, Allison benefited from the support she received from her family.

Reflection Point 2.3

Meaningful communication with parents involves more than information sharing. Think about components that encourage parents to support their children's learning in a way that is consistent with school instruction and expectations. Design a one-page, parent-friendly flier for this purpose. Consider including tips for time management, ways to eliminate distractions, points to emphasize the value of rereading, and an invitation to visit your classroom.

Our First One-to-One Lesson

Based on my observations during exploration sessions, I was able to plan pertinent instruction for Allison. I had observed that she already used more letter sounds appropriately in her writing than she had in her assessments. In addition, neatness seemed to be very important to her. She repeatedly erased letters until they met her approval. I was also aware that she was a quiet child who did not seem comfortable taking risks. She did not volunteer information unless she was certain she was correct. Because I knew that a risk-taking climate was necessary for Allison—or any student—to grow as Kohn states, the "higher-level, creative, and experimental thought" (as cited in Costa, 1987, p.11) required to read, I knew I had to develop a base of trust.

Reflection Point 2.4

When working with a child who is reluctant to take risks, it is a constant struggle to know how to divide instructional time between reinforcing understood concepts and offering new pertinent instruction. Identify a student in your class who is fearful of taking risks. For the next few weeks, keep a record of how you divide your time between reinforcement and new learning with this child. Are there fluctuations? List possible reasons for spending more or less time on reinforcement on any given day.

As our first one-on-one lesson proceeded, I offered Allison choices from several books that I felt she might be comfortable reading. From these books, Allison selected a teacher-made copy of *Twinkle, Twinkle Little Star*, one of her favorite books because a window in each page allows the reader to view the star. Allison had memorized this nursery rhyme, but as she "read" it, I became aware that she did not match her voice to the print. To help her with this, I asked her to find the word *star* on the first page. We continued through the book, identifying a specific word on each page. Then, I offered to read the entire book with her as she pointed to each word. Her next selection was *Little Pig to Market*, another familiar nursery rhyme. During this reading, Allison pointed to each word as she read slowly and haltingly through the text, demonstrating voice–print correspondence.

Then we moved on to the next component of the LEAP lesson—word study. During word study, Allison would receive additional experience with individual words to clarify her understanding of this concept.

Word Study With Allison

Mrs. Germain and I chose six words as our focus for the small group's four-day lesson plan for the week: *a, at, as, and, can,* and *had.* Based on the students' needs, we planned pertinent instruction so students would focus on these words in the LEAP classroom and the regular classroom. We selected words that would provide the most gain for the most students. Allison had used these words in word wall activities during her previous session with Mrs. Germain.

During the session, Allison's group played "Be a Mind Reader," in which students had to listen to Mrs. Germain's clues to determine which word she was thinking of. Therefore, I provided the magnetic letters *a, t, s, n, d,* and *c* for Allison to move to form words I dictated. In her first attempt to form *can,* Allison ordered the letters *acn.* Following my prompt to reread the word, she quickly self-corrected the word. "I know that word. I was just too fast!" she explained. I then used a "mix-fix" strategy, mixing the letters again and asking her to make the word. Next, Allison successfully wrote the six words on a white board as I dictated them to her. "These words are easy for me now!" she exclaimed.

For Allison's new book selection, I chose *Moms and Dads* (Randell, Giles, & Smith, 1996c) from the Reading Recovery level 1 basket. I felt Allison had shown understanding of voice–print correspondence and was able to use the strong picture clues to cross-check with the initial sounds of words in this text. In her first attempt to read the book, she substituted *vet* for *veterinarian.* I used this opportunity to discuss word length. I asked, "What would the word *vet* look like?" "Oops! *Vet* would be a short word," Allison replied. She then quickly responded with the correct word.

Reflection Point 2.5

Vocabulary knowledge is critical to students' success. How would you approach words such as *veterinarian* or *vet* with a student who lacks any knowledge of these words? Examine five reading selections. Make a list of words that could be challenging. What could you do to clarify them?

Making Family Connections

I like to have my students begin individual lessons by rereading familiar books. This provides a warm-up to reading with an independent-level book. This also gives students time to physically and mentally calm down. It is especially important for groups coming directly from recess. These books then provide prompts for writing in draft books. During individual lessons with Allison, I generally used a previously read book as the prompt for her writing in the draft book. After reading *Moms and Dads*, Allison chose to write about her mother. She carefully considered the length of the sentences she was composing: "My mom's job is to take care of my three sisters and me. She stays at home. That's what I want to say, but it is too many words to write," she remarked. Allison had counted the words on her fingers as she spoke them. Her facial expression reflected her concern that this was beyond both her writing ability and her patience. I asked her if she could think of another way to tell about her mother's job. She paused and said, "My Mom stays at home with my littlest sister. She doesn't go to work. What do you call that?" I replied that there were several titles people used for that job, such as housewife, parent, homemaker, and full-time mother. Allison slowly considered these options and finally said, "I think I'll write 'Mom is a house mom.'" (See Figure 2 for Allison's sentence written in her draft book.)

Mom was a word Allison had written in her Writing Vocabulary assessment. However, at first she reversed the *s* as she wrote the word *is*. I asked her to check it with the *s* on the alphabet strip on our table. Then, we used white correction tape as a Band-Aid to cover the incorrect letter,

Figure 2
Draft Book Page

and Allison corrected this word. Next, Allison used the top of the page in her draft book, our "practice area," to write *house* (see Figure 3). Allison wrote an *h*. After confirming the accuracy of the first sound, I asked her to think about the rest of the sounds of the word. Allison and I used our hands to show how we "stretch" the word as we sound it out. Then, I drew Elkonin sound boxes on the practice area. Allison counted the boxes and repeated the sounds of the word as a check. I incorporated pertinent instruction by showing Allison that two letters often make one sound. Allison continued stretching the word to add the *s*, and I let her know that this word had a silent *e* on the end. She then copied the word in the correct place in her sentence and ended the sentence with *mom* and a period. Allison was proud to reread the final correct version of the sentence she had chosen to write.

For another experience with these words, I then wrote Allison's sentence on a paper sentence strip and cut between each word. Allison had no difficulty reassembling and rereading the sentence. I sent the pieces home in a small plastic bag with an instruction sheet to guide her parents as they practiced this activity with her. When parents are provided with an activity and specific instructions, students are able to receive consistent support at home.

As our lesson was ending, Allison and I read a paper take-home copy of *Old McDonald Had a Farm*. I observed that she again carefully matched each word she spoke with the written words. I placed this book in Allison's green pocket along with a reminder to put it in her book box at home. Finally, I wrote a brief note to Allison's parents relating a point

Figure 3
Draft Book Practice Page

from our lesson and suggesting they encourage Allison to use her fingers to match written words to spoken words when she read at home. I wanted this home support to be consistent with our work at school.

Early Progress

By the end of September, Allison and I had met for two more one-on-one lessons. She now consistently showed understanding of voice–print correspondence. Although Allison was primarily using picture clues to figure out unknown words, she was starting to cross-check these words by looking for initial letter–sound correspondence. Another observation I made was that she stayed with a word until she was sure it was correct.

In the book *Bump, Bump, Bump* (Wood, 1997), Allison did not know what the pictured wheelbarrow was, so she used letter sounds. She repeated every sound for each letter in this word twice and then asked, "What is that thing? I have seen one at my grandparents' house, but I don't know what they call it. I think it might be a wheel something." Allison seemed relieved when I read the compound word, pointing out *wheel*. The word *fell* was another challenge for Allison in this text. She was uncertain of the sound for *e*, so she substituted the word *went* to make sense in the sentence. However, she quickly admitted, "That's not right because the word starts with the /f/ sound." Allison was thinking about her reading and using multiple strategies, which I attributed to my pertinent instruction.

As she worked in her draft book, Allison wrote *hv* for *have*, asked for a correction tape band-aid, then moved to the practice area of the page and wrote *hav*. She referred to the previously read book to correctly write the word. These gains, not yet made by two students in her group, led me to believe Allison was ready for books from the next Reading Recovery level, which offered more challenges.

Struggles

Our next individual lesson was one of many struggles. Allison began by choosing familiar books from the level 1 basket. She chose *Dads* (Randell, Giles, & Smith, 1996a), *Moms and Dads* (Randell et al., 1996c), and *Good Morning* (Horn, 1998). She read these books successfully and commented on the similarities between the books *Dads* and *Moms and Dads*. We checked and confirmed that the same authors wrote both books.

During the word study portion of the lesson, Allison used magnetic letters to form dictated words.

Allison: [touching the magnetic letters] /g/-/e/-/t/. That's *get*.

Bev: Allison, now change the *g* to a *w*. What word does that make?

Allison: /w/-/e/-/t/. That says *wet*.

Bev: What word is it if the *w* is changed to a *p*?

Allison: /p/-/e/-/t/, *pet*.

Bev: We can make a lot of words by changing just the first sound. Try taking away the *p* and replacing it with *s*.

Allison: /s/-/e/-/t/, set. Now it says *set*.

Bev: Let's try another. Please change the *s* to an *l*.

Allison: /l/-/e/-/t/, *let*.

Bev: This will be the last word. Change the *l* to *m*.

Allison: /m/-/e/-/t/, *met*.

Bev: Allison, let's practice all those words again by writing them on the white board. What is a good color of marker for you to use today?

Allison: I think I'd like to use an orange marker today. Last time I used purple, and I want to use purple in my draft book today because it is my favorite color.

[As I dictate the words, Allison writes them accurately on the white board. She again says each sound as she writes the words.]

Bev: Allison, would you use this green marker to underline the last sound in each word?

Allison: Yes. All the words end with *t*!

Bev: Now would you underline the vowel in each word?

Allison: OK. They all have *e* in them! So all the words have an *e* and a *t* at the end!

Bev: Now would you read each word again?

Allison: /g/-/e/-/t/, get; /w/-/e/-/t/, wet; /p/-/e/-/t/, pet; /s/-/e/-/t/, set.

[Allison continues down the column of words, saying the sound for each letter.]

Bev: Allison, you told me that all the words end with *e* followed by *t*. We say that as /et/. I can read these words without sounding them out because we know what /et/ says. They say *get*, *wet*, *pet*, *set*, *let*, and *met*. Give it a try.

Allison: Do I have to? These words are boring.

Bev: Let's read them quickly together.

Allison's struggle and frustration using rimes surprised me. I thought this was a concept she understood. Now I, too, wanted to move to an area for success so I replied, "Let's go back to the book we read last time. It had really colorful illustrations."

To change the activity, we went on to reread *Bumps, Bumps, Bumps* from the previous lesson. In this rereading, Allison substituted *went* for *fell* each time she encountered it. The final sentence was, "How many things fell out?" As Allison read the sentence, she carefully moved her finger from word to word saying, "'Where...did...all...the...stuff...go?' That isn't right! I'm too tired to think today." Allison's struggles had clouded her purpose of decoding words.

Reflection Point 2.6

The reality is that we all have "off" days. Share any successes you have had turning students around on a day like this. What do you do to combat off days? Discuss your responses with some colleagues. Together, compile a list of strategies to use in these situations.

Working without an off-day list, I gave Allison the magnetic letters *e*, *f*, *l*, and *l* and asked her what she thought the word *fell* would look like. She correctly formed the word. We then went back to the text and identified the word *fell* in the text. Allison seemed pleased with this success.

Then, it was time to compose a sentence from the story. Allison was not interested in this activity, however. "I don't really like this story. I don't want to write about it. Is it almost time to go back to Ms. Peters's class?" she asked. Because of her struggles with the text, Allison lost any sense of purpose for writing. I suggested several sentences, but she rejected them quickly. Finally she decided to write, *The street had lots of bumps*. Allison wrote *setrt* for *street*. We used sound boxes on the practice area to correct this error. Allison wrote *los* for *lots* so we counted the sounds as we stretched out this word and corrected it. I modeled *of* and suggested Allison copy *bumps* from the book title. I copied Allison's sentence onto a sentence strip and cut the words apart. Allison quickly reassembled this sentence.

I possibly learned more during this lesson than Allison. I noted that to maintain a sense of purpose Allison needed to have many successes and few challenges in lessons. As we worked together in later lessons, sentence composition continued to be a challenge for her. She did not want to attempt unknown words, so she carefully chose a sentence containing only familiar words. The sentences Allison wrote in her group lessons often repeated successes in our individual lessons. I determined Allison needed continued consistent support to experience more growth.

I also observed that incidents in the lunchroom and on the playground often carried over into our LEAP sessions. Taking a few minutes for meaningful conversation to discuss these events allowed Allison to move on with the lesson and concentrate better.

More Progress

In November, I noticed Allison was primarily using letter sounds to decode unknown words and did not seem to use the picture clues or predicting strategies as she had used in previous lessons. To emphasize these strategies, I selected the book *Kitty and the Birds* (Randell, 1996e) for her new read. Allison and I discussed the relationship between birds and cats and predicted possible problems. She expressed her dislike of cats and her interest in dogs and her pet snake. She felt her snake also might like to eat birds but would not be able to catch them as a cat could. Our meaningful conversation led Allison to engage with the book and to make connections with her own personal experiences. If she had read this story alone, this may not have taken place.

As she read the text, the words *hungry, comes, safe, down,* and *meow* were challenges. I noted that pertinent instruction would be necessary to solve these words. With a few prompts, Allison worked to use meaning and word patterns to successfully read this text. We worked on using context clues for meaning. For example, Allison read past the unknown word and used picture clues to read the word *down*. As she came to the word *safe*, she ignored the silent *e* as she said the letter sounds. She had practiced the silent final *e* generalization both in LEAP and in her classroom word study activities. I asked her if she had seen other words with an *e* on the end. She looked puzzled and asked for an example. I knew many of her draft book sentences contained the word *like*, so I opened her book to a page with the word on it. She read her entry and then reread the sentence in the story and pronounced *safe* correctly. This opportunity for pertinent instruction allowed me to use the word *like*, which Allison already could spell as a sight word, to take her to a new understanding of word patterns for reading. At the end of our lesson, we reviewed thinking about the illustrations and context clues to help with difficult words.

Allison's Need for Consistent Support

By the middle of November, it was time to assess our LEAP students again. These quarterly assessments included many of the original tests and the additions of an oral reading analysis of classroom material and comprehension questions about the same selection.

Based on the November assessment results (refer to Table 1 on page 21), Mrs. Germain and I were pleased to note Allison's improved knowledge of letter sounds and her inclusion of correct vowel sounds in her writing. She had confidence to write 34 words. The oral reading analysis of an unread classroom selection, *I Like Cats* (Kahn, 1996), a Watch Me Read title from the Houghton Mifflin series, showed this text was clearly at frustration level for Allison. Her reading miscues reflected that she continued to depend on letter sounds in 23 attempts. I was surprised to realize she had self-corrected 15 times in this reading—possibly due to our work on cross-checking. Allison struggled with high-frequency words. I noted she had not reread at any time in this selection; rereading would be an area for future instruction. Her struggle to respond correctly to the comprehension questions matched her struggle to read the text.

When I shared these results with Allison's classroom teacher, Ms. Peters shared her concern with Allison's reluctance to write and her poor use of time during the writing block in the classroom. I agreed to support the classroom goals by using activities in our LEAP sessions to emphasize strategies to improve Allison's use of time and to develop her confidence in writing. Ms. Peters was pleasantly surprised with Allison's success in the Dictation Task and her ability to read 79% of the words in the story. I encouraged her to give Allison more opportunities to read in class. This exchange of ideas served to strengthen the instruction we offered Allison both in the classroom and in LEAP.

I found that lunch break in the teachers' dining room also provided an important opportunity to share observations of students and to exchange instructional ideas with Mrs. Germain and the classroom teachers. We discussed recent student successes and struggles and reflected on them. We often planned classroom activities. Mrs. Germain and I also escorted our LEAP groups to and from their classrooms, so we often briefly connected with the classroom teachers in these encounters. Each week the classroom teachers provided us with a copy of their word study lists and reading selections. These important connections to provide consistent support for our students depended greatly on everyone's continued efforts to communicate.

During our instruction in the LEAP classroom, we primarily used books at the students' reading levels. However, to support classroom work, Mrs. Germain's lessons included prereading stories from classroom anthologies. These readings became the basis for activities to teach comprehension skills. Because of these activities, our LEAP students often were very familiar with the stories when they were used in the regular classroom. This familiarity encouraged Allison and her group to respond successfully to discussion questions in class. However, students in several LEAP groups complained to us that they never had opportunities to participate in discussions in their regular classrooms. When I asked the teachers about these comments, they stated that they chose not to call on our LEAP students because of these prior experiences. These classroom teachers felt that prior reading gave the LEAP students an unfair advantage. The LEAP program, on the other hand, recognizes the importance of prior reading for struggling students. This difference in philosophies interfered with offering consistent support. Therefore, we explained our reasons for prereading and discussing stories ahead of time and encouraged classroom teachers to involve LEAP students in at least part of the classroom discussions.

Reflection Point 2.7

When there is a difference in philosophies between a classroom teacher and a reading support program, the student is the potential loser. Create a list of questions to guide discussions on reading philosophies. For example, what current research supports your philosophy? How does the student benefit from your philosophy?

Half-Way Point of the Year

For the final LEAP session of the first semester, Allison reread the book *Where Are You Going, Aja Rose?* (Cowley, 1996d) with 97% accuracy. She quickly decided to write, *I have lots of friends* in her draft book. She used sound boxes to construct the words *lots* and *friends*. She wrote *of* on the practice area of the page. She asked me, "Is that right?"

In return, I asked her, "Does it look right to you?" She decided it did but then checked the Word Wall for verification.

I selected *Lucky Goes to Dog School* (Randell, 1996f), a level 7 book, for the new story, knowing that Allison would easily connect with it because she frequently wrote about her dogs. She immediately compared the illustration of Lucky to her dogs. As she "picture walked," or scanned the illustrations, through this book, she confidently predicted the problem in the story:

> We never let my dogs go in the street. A car might hit them! I didn't know dogs could go to school. That is a good idea to teach dogs to be good. One of my dogs never listens to my mom, but it does mind my dad.

I did not want Allison to feel unnecessarily frustrated in our lesson, so before reading, I introduced the names of the characters in the story. Allison located them in the text. As she read, she found the word *naughty* challenging. She first tried letter sounds. Then, she automatically reread the page. I suggested she finish the page and then try a word that made sense. "The only word that makes sense to me is *bad* and it can't be *bad*." I asked her what she had heard her parents call her dog when it didn't follow directions. She considered this and suggested *bad* again. After another hesitation she asked, "Could that word be *naughty*? My Grandma says my little sister is naughty when she tears books." By being provided with wait time, Allison was able to successfully solve this word. Research supports the power of providing wait time; Rowe (as cited in Good & Brophy, 1999) found in a study of good questioning techniques that "longer wait times led to more active participation in lessons by a larger percentage of the students coupled with an increase in the quality of the participation" (p. 393).

When we finished reading the story, I asked Allison if she would like to read it again together. She agreed, so we took turns reading by pages. As I added expression to my portion, she did, too. As I read a little faster, she also did. This was a successful lesson for Allison. She wrote a sentence nearly independently, an area of focus in our efforts to offer consistent support, and, due to pertinent instruction, she was able to use reading strategies to solve words and to begin working to improve her reading fluency. Allison seemed to recognize the purpose for her efforts.

A Break in the Routine

Then, due to winter recess, we did not have another LEAP session for more than two weeks. These long breaks in our routine produced interesting results. Some students, including Allison, seemed truly refreshed with new enthusiasm for school and learning when we returned. However, other students returned seeming to have lost many skills. Allison proudly reported she had spent much of the vacation in Flagstaff, Arizona, with her grandparents. They had played in the snow—a real treat for children living in the desert. Her grandparents also had given her several books for holiday gifts and made time to read with her daily.

We were hesitant our first year to send books home over the long vacation, fearing they would be lost. However, now we choose to take this risk to help parents of LEAP students continue to support their children's reading growth with appropriate reading materials. This is part of providing for consistent support. In addition, we include a note offering suggested reading and writing activities with our holiday gifts to students—books, of course!

Reflection Point 2.8

Many parents view reading as a school-based activity, so vacations from school mean vacations from reading. Parents are reading every day, though—in the kitchen, the grocery store, and the workshop, and while driving, choosing television programs, and even while waiting in lines or in the doctor's office. Create a flier for parents showing how they can involve their children in these home literacy experiences. How can teachers make better connections to these home literacy experiences in the classroom?

Allison Finds Her Purpose

Following our return from vacation, Ms. Peters and I met and decided Laura—one of Allison's friends in the group—was ready to exit the LEAP program. After making the decision to exit Laura, I discussed this with her during our next individual lesson. We talked about the strategies she now used to read well and of how proud Ms. Peters, Laura's parents, Mrs. Germain, and I were of her success. Laura also selected a treat to share at her graduation celebration—doughnuts. Laura was delighted with her success and with the attention she received during her graduation celebration. Allison seemed envious of Laura's success and expressed that she would miss her friend. Now Allison seemed especially determined to graduate, too. At this time, Carl joined the LEAP group, filling the spot that Laura had vacated.

We scheduled assessments for the end of January to provide current information of each student's abilities to share at the next parent–teacher conference meetings. As my session with Allison began, she asked if she would graduate if she did well on the tests. She seemed especially motivated but also more frustrated when challenged by new tasks.

The January assessments showed growth for Allison in her use of high-frequency words. She read 18 words on the Ohio Word Test. Her writing vocabulary included 44 single-syllable words with 6 incorrect attempts. This list included many names of Allison's family members. The classroom selection for the Oral Reading Analysis was another Houghton Mifflin Watch Me Read book, *Grasshopper and Ant* (Haber, 1996). Ms. Peters had planned to use this book for instruction the next week so Allison had not yet read it. She read this selection with 98% accuracy, which is at the independent-level reading. Her reading did not sound fluent because she self-corrected seven times (refer to Table 1 on page 21). Allison was very proud of her success and repeated her question, "Will I get to graduate from LEAP soon?"

Providing More Pertinent Instruction

Our next individual lesson offered several unanticipated opportunities for pertinent instruction. After rereading several familiar books, we continued with our word study that included the two-syllable word *quiet*. Allison wrote *quit* on a marker board. When I asked her to read her word, she responded, "Oops! That is the word *quit*. I must have left something out." We then stretched the sounds of the word and clapped for each syllable. For additional practice with *quiet*, Allison wrote the word five times, in the middle of the marker board and in each of the four corners. We describe this as "four corners" practice. I prompted each repetition to be a little faster to encourage automaticity. Allison then read aloud *quiet* as she erased each attempt.

After I took an oral reading analysis of Allison's reading of the book *Hermit Crab* (Randell, 1996d) from our previous lesson, she shared her plan to write, *There are fish that eat hermit crabs*. However, she actually wrote, *There's a fish that eats hermit crabs*. As she finished her composition, I asked her to read it to me. She read this sentence as written. I asked her if she had planned to write those words. She looked at her writing and excitedly explained, "Today Ms. Peters showed us how to put words together. I can't remember what you call it, but you put a flying comma thing where some letters are missing. Then you don't have to write so much!" I had not anticipated this opportunity to teach this use of apostrophes but decided to provide support with a lesson on contractions. I affirmed Allison's description of contractions and provided the correct name for the "flying comma"—the apostrophe. We checked our word wall for other contractions and Allison added two contractions: *can't* and *don't*.

Hoping to help her recall her original idea for the sentence, I opened the book to the page with an illustration showing a fish threatening the hermit crab. I asked Allison if she thought there was only one fish interested in eating the hermit crab. She carefully thought and replied, "No, there are lots of fish in the ocean. I don't know if they all like to eat crabs." I asked her what she could write to tell a reader that many fish tried to eat the crab. She replied, "I could say 'There are fish that like to eat hermit crabs.'" Then she looked at me and said, "That's what I told you I would write, isn't it? I guess I changed my mind or forgot."

I originally had selected *Baby Bear's Present* (Randell, 1994) as the new book and had planned to model possessives; however, because Allison had been working on apostrophes in her classroom, I decided pertinent instruction for that day would be limited to the correct name for this punctuation mark and its use in contractions. After predicting events from the illustrations and connecting this book with a previous story, Allison read *Baby Bear's Present* nearly fluently. She reread a sentence to correct and carefully considered picture clues. She retold this story and identified the problem and the solution clearly. Her retelling lacked an introduction, so it seemed pertinent to discuss this element.

To offer an experience with an introduction, we pretended it was the first time we met—when Allison came to our classroom for testing. We introduced ourselves. Then, we looked at the book and read the first page again. We decided this book did not have a good introduction, but we already knew the characters from reading other books by this author. Allison suggested, "'Once upon a time' would be a good introduction because this was not a real story." When I asked if she might include an introduction when she retold a story she added, "That would make it sound more like a real book!"

Our recent assessments had shown that Allison was now able to read more high-frequency words. This also was reflected in her increased reading accuracy. I planned to apply this knowledge to decoding multisyllabic words, possessives, and contractions. I also wanted to guide Allison to expand her retelling skills and improve her fluency through repeated reading opportunities. Allison was experiencing significant growth.

Flowers Everywhere: Publishing Allison's Writing

Every year, Mrs. Germain and I enjoy having each student write a story to be published. These "real books" give students a purpose to their writing (see Box 2.2 for resources on publishing student work). I read aloud Jamie Lee Curtis's book *When I Was Little: A Four-Year-Old's Memoir of*

Box 2.2
Resources for Publishing Student Work

Calkins, L.M. (1994). *The art of teaching writing.* Portsmouth, NH: Heinemann.

Evans, J., & Moore, J.E. (1988). *How to make books with children.* Monterey, CA: Evan-Moor.

Jordan, K., & Adsit, K. (2004). *Bookmaking bonanza: Creative bookmaking ideas to motivate beginning readers and writers.* Huntington Beach, CA: Creative Teaching Press.

Morrow, L.M. (2002). *The literacy center: Contexts for reading and writing* (2nd ed.). Portland, ME: Stenhouse.

Ray, K.W. (with Cleaveland, L.B.). (2004). *About the authors: Writing workshop with our youngest writers.* Portsmouth, NH: Heinemann.

Her Youth (1995) as a model of a book developed from a simple topic with which the students can easily identify. We all enjoy laughing at the silly things the young girl did. I reread the introduction and conclusion to emphasize the important story elements. Then, our students write and illustrate their own stories. We supply sheets of paper with boxes printed on the upper half for illustrations done with black fine-point markers and a few lines on the lower half for writing the text. To make the books look authentic, I type the text and tape it over the student-written text. Then, these pages are copied, folded, and stapled.

These publications provide high-interest reading materials for our students and an opportunity for each student author to be recognized. Mrs. Germain and I select a student's book to feature each day and that student becomes the "Author of the Day." The authors wear special stickers to identify themselves and read their books orally to the students in the group. Every LEAP student receives a copy of the featured book to add to their book boxes at home. Students spend the first few minutes of our session reading and discussing the positive features of each book.

Allison struggled to select a topic as she began her book. After writing a page, she changed her mind several times. She wrote a sentence about her snake but tossed this aside. "Everybody knows about my snake!" she exclaimed. Recalling the flowers she brought to school for her teacher, she finally decided to write about flowers. She called her book *Flowers Everywhere* (see Figure 4).

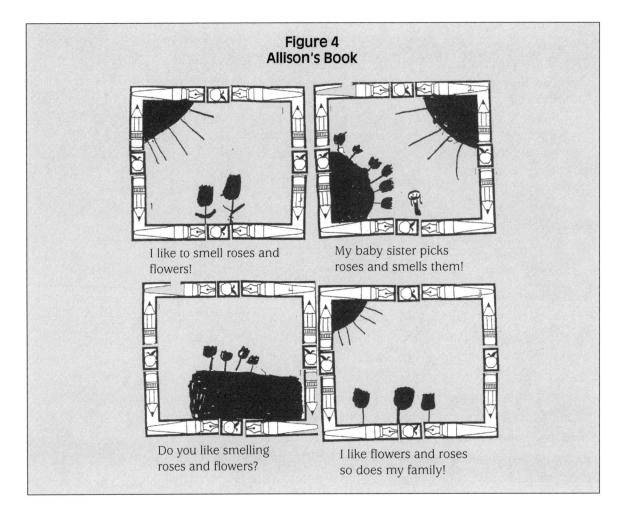

Figure 4
Allison's Book

I like to smell roses and flowers!

My baby sister picks roses and smells them!

Do you like smelling roses and flowers?

I like flowers and roses so does my family!

When Allison was the featured author, her book prompted meaningful conversation. Beth promptly shared her expert opinion that at her parents' nursery the "roses smell the best!" Robert asked if Allison's little sister had been "poked by the thorns" as he had been. At Carl's suggestion, the group asked to take a moment to add color to the illustrations. Allison was pleased with her friends' responses to her book, especially the suggestion to enhance her illustrations. Allison learned that she could share her ideas with her classmates and receive valuable feedback.

Accepting Challenges

When Allison and I next worked together, she was very comfortable writing rhyming words as I dictated them as a word-study activity. Her new book was *The Giant Gingerbread Man* (Feely, 1999a) from our level 9 basket. This text uses 243 words. This text length was a new challenge for Allison in LEAP sessions, although certainly she had encountered lengthy text in other situations. She had recognized the word count number inside the front cover and was amazed and proud to read a book with so many words. Following her first reading of this story, we took the opportunity to compare and contrast it with a more familiar version of the story (Schmidt, 1967).

A week later, after rereading this story, Allison wrote *I like decurateng gingerbread men* in her draft book. As she suggested this sentence, we checked her previous entries to avoid beginning the sentence in the same manner as other entries. "I like" is an often-used sentence starter, but she had not used it for the past six entries so we agreed it was acceptable. I observed that Allison had substituted *-eng* for *-ing* and noted this substitution as a possible basis for pertinent instruction for when we would select our words for next week. Then, I selected a new book that offered another opportunity for comparison with a traditional version.

Mr. Wolf Tries Again (Prince, 1999) interested Allison immediately as she examined the cover illustration of a wolf in a black leather jacket standing beside a motorcycle. As she read, I noted she repeated sections to self-correct. She seemed to use meaning and to monitor her reading. She asked to read this story again to her family. Planning to use this goal as a motivator, I suggested she practice it again in our next sessions before taking the book home.

During our next session, Allison accurately read this book and successfully responded to it. Her reading included four repetitions, two hesitations, and five self-corrections. These hindered her fluency. We reread her favorite parts of this book to add expression and increase the rate of reading. Because she chose the sections to read, Allison seemed happy to read the book again. I added expression by reading the wolf dialogue in my best wolf voice, and Allison hesitantly did the same. Her feelings of enthusiasm and confidence were reflected in her sentence in her draft book. Allison wrote, *The big bad wolf thought he could catch the three pigs!* This entry had more words than any previous entry. Her choice of the word *thought* was a surprising change from her usual choice of familiar words.

I chose *Harry's House* (Medearis, 1994), a level 10 book, as Allison's next new book because it was about dogs, one of Allison's favorite topics, and because it included an obvious problem and solution plot, a story element I wanted to encourage Allison to include as she retold stories. Allison carefully examined the illustrations and predicted the problem and its solution. She read the text slowly as she examined the details in the illustrations. She substituted several sight words but self-corrected to reflect the meaning of the story. Again, Allison asked, "Am I getting closer to graduating?" I assured her she was but that I wanted her to stay for a little while longer to practice reading like we talk. I shared this in my note to her mother with the addition that I wanted to give Allison time to be more confident in her use of strategies and to improve her fluency. This information enabled Allison's family to offer consistent support. In fact, Allison's mother responded that she agreed and would focus on fluency through rereading at home.

Allison wrote an interesting entry in her draft book during her next session with Mrs. Germain. Remember, the RIA offers little support during these writing sessions so that she can gather diagnostic information. As students complete their entries, Mrs. Germain gives them a moment to stand and read their sentences to the two other group members. Often, this oral reading alerts the writer to errors in sentence structure and meaning. Allison's entry, *My favorite food is peanut butter and fluff*, produced loud groans from her friends (see Figure 5). Her entry prompted meaningful conversation and provided students with a better understanding of the purpose of their writing.

Robert: I've never heard of fluff! I do like peanut butter, but what is fluff?

Allison: It's fluff. You know—white stuff like clouds.

Mrs. Germain: Allison, do you mean marshmallow cream? It's white, tastes very sweet like marshmallows, and comes in a jar?

**Figure 5
Draft Book Entry**

Allison:	Yes! That's it! Fluff.
Carl:	[quietly to me] That sounds disgusting!
Robert:	That still sounds weird! Peanut butter is good. Why add the fluff stuff?

[Allison assured Robert he would like it and seemed very proud of introducing us to a new food.]

Following Allison's "fluff" entry was an attempt at poetry (see Figure 6). This was a variation from Allison's usual entries of a sentence about one of her interests or a planned activity, and it was a unique entry for this group. Allison was obviously feeling more confident about her skills as a writer.

Mrs. Germain encouraged the students to choose topics for their writing. She usually asked each student to share the planned sentence with her orally before writing to prevent repeated or inappropriate entries. Occasionally, a student's written sentence varied from the originally planned sentence due to that student's comfort with word spellings, distractions during writing, grammatical confusions, or forgetfulness.

Figure 6
Draft Book Poem

The variety of topics selected and the length of these entries reflected the students' interests, known vocabulary, personality, and willingness to take risks. Students often imitated successful entries. Therefore, in reaction to this repetition of sentences and lists of favorite characters or family members, Mrs. Germain and I developed guidelines for entries:

- Each entry must be different.
- Sentences cannot start the same way more than three times.
- Sentences cannot be like your friends' sentences.

Students often looked back at their early entries with disbelief. They shared reactions such as "I didn't write messy like that!" "Can I fix this word? It isn't spelled right!" "I wrote the same thing lots of times!" Because they show students' progress, these draft books can be treasured as records of a year of growth for these children. Allison's draft book was evidence of her growth in writing.

During her next individual lesson, as Allison reread *Harry's House*, she seemed to attempt "to read like we talk," reading the text quickly and making errors. She substituted *in* for *on*, *off* for *out*, and *how* for *now*. She did self-correct 10 words quickly, but we were both discouraged. We took turns reading a portion of the story again at a slower, yet appropriate, rate for success. To encourage fluency, I selected a new book at the same level. Allison attempted to read the word *ready* using letter sounds and sentence structure cues. She also self-corrected meaningful substitutions for *then* and *with*. I complimented her for using these strategies. She asked if she could take home additional books for practice to help her graduate. We decided she could read the two books from her pocket several times and have time to do her homework from Ms. Peters.

Celebrating Success—Graduation

Allison began the next lesson by reading three books from the level 9 basket, the level I determined to be her independent level. Our word study focused on the /kn/ phonogram in *knew*. She wrote on the white board the words I dictated and read them as she erased each word. An oral analysis of her reading of *Socks Off!* (Lang, 1999), a level 9 book, showed 97% accuracy with four repetitions and seven self-corrections. I noted she read this book at an appropriate rate. In addition, after reading this book Allison decided to write *I like to play games* in her draft book and was successful.

Following her choppy experience in our previous lesson, I had selected *Tarantula* (Feely, 1999b) from level 11 as an opportunity for her to improve her fluency using a nonfiction book. Allison shared her knowledge of a surprising number of facts about these creatures and enthusiasm for this topic. She had few difficulties with this text and used a variety of strategies to solve unknown words. This lesson seemed to be a solid indicator of her readiness to exit LEAP. She was excited and proud of her success.

Following this lesson, I had many questions to consider. I wondered if I had offered Allison enough challenges in this lesson. Had I allowed her to succeed to please her and to validate the success of this support program? How long would she maintain her enthusiasm to reach her goal of graduation from LEAP? Had prior experience led me to support Allison? Was I doing the best for her long-term success in reading?

Ms. Peters and I met to discuss Allison's progress toward exiting from LEAP. Ms. Peters shared that Allison now often volunteered to read the books from her green pocket to her classmates during her turn in the Reader's Chair, a special chair in the classroom reserved for a student who is reading to the group. Composition was still an area of concern as Allison continued to use a great deal of the allotted time getting started. Ms. Peters completed an oral reading analysis on classroom material to compare Allison's abilities with those of other students. Allison read the selection as well as half of her classmates did, suggesting she would be an average reader in her classroom.

Knowing that Allison's mother would continue daily reading practice with the books from LEAP gave us more confidence in our decision to exit Allison from LEAP. Allison would continue to place her green pocket in the crate each morning for new books from the LEAP library. Ms. Peters would continue to communicate with me about Allison's progress so I could provide books at the appropriate level. Therefore, even though Allison might no longer be participating in the LEAP lessons, consistent support would be provided.

During our next individual lesson, I told Allison of the decision to exit her from the program and allow her to select her treat for this celebration. As I shared the news with Allison, she was ecstatic. She rushed through the rereading selection, making careless errors—not a reassuring response! However, she did add expression during her reading of a new selection. Our teaching point had been to focus on phrasing, and she was eager to be successful. She asked to read several sections again to practice this idea.

Then, Allison spent much time on her big decision of the day—selecting a snack for her celebration. Allison considered peanut butter and "fluff" sandwiches but eliminated them when she recalled Robert's reaction to the description of this favorite food. I reminded her of Laura's choice of doughnuts. As in her decision-making process for compositions, Allison slowly considered many logical choices and several unusual options before she selected hot wings. Her chosen treat was our secret until her celebration the next week.

Follow-Up

I continued to see Allison nearly daily the following year. She seemed to be a happy second-grade student with many friends. I often met her on her way to the school library to select books. When Mrs. Germain and I met with the second-grade teachers to select students for brief tutoring sessions, I first asked about the former LEAP students. Allison's teacher was amazed that Allison had participated in LEAP. Although she was not the best reader in her class, Allison was considered a very competent reader by her teacher. She still talked about her snake and she often brought peanut butter and "fluff" sandwiches in her lunch!

Conclusion

Allison's journey in LEAP was successful. Once she discovered a purpose of her own for making an effort to read, I was able to use the points of action effectively. Allison's choices enabled me to determine what instruction would be pertinent and helped me set purposes for lessons. Reading her original sentences, sharing her own books, and participating in other meaningful conversations allowed her to grow as a reader. One of the most powerful points of action leading to Allison's reading success was the consistent support she received from her family, which was cooperative and involved. My journey continues as I use the points of action to lead other struggling young readers to discover the world of literacy.

Chapter 3

A Year With Joshua: Growth in Communication and Confidence

Joshua enters Kathleen's LEAP classroom one day early in fall.
  Kathleen: Joshua, did you bring your books to LEAP today?
  Joshua: Huh?

Joshua appears unable to focus on the question, although his facial expression indicates that he realizes I am speaking to him.
  Kathleen: Joshua, did you bring your books to LEAP today?
  Joshua: Oh.... Yes...they are in my backpack.

When Joshua first entered my classroom, I was surprised. I had worked with his brother in the LEAP program and had had the opportunity to meet Joshua at parent–teacher conferences as well as before and after school when his mother occasionally visited. In these situations in which both boys were present, they moved quickly, they did not follow directions well, and they changed their activities rapidly. Therefore, I anticipated a far more active and assertive personality from Joshua.

However, Joshua was quiet, reserved, and hesitant. He seldom initiated conversation or responded spontaneously to it. Getting him to respond to questions usually required more than one request. Immediately questions arose in my mind: Did he understand our questions? Was it difficult for him to express himself?

Joshua had attended our school's kindergarten program as well as the kindergarten enrichment program the previous year. Even though these experiences had offered Joshua opportunities to develop greater language skills, he was far from being ready to be a successful first grader. His kindergarten teachers indicated that he was a student who might benefit from LEAP intervention in first grade. Therefore, he was automatically included in the initial screening assessments.

Reflection Point 3.1 _____

Teachers often have prior knowledge of students and/or their families before they actually meet them. This knowledge can come from other teachers, the students' siblings, or student records. How does prior knowledge about a student affect your thinking and your expectations? Create a T-chart to show the advantages and disadvantages of having prior knowledge of a student.

Initial Assessments

The results of Joshua's initial screening assessments in September were encouraging (see Table 2). Joshua already could identify 45 of 54 letters on the Letter Identification assessment, which placed him at stanine 1. All of his responses were alphabetic names rather than letter sounds or words beginning with specific letters. Confusions included the following: U-W, R-O, W-Q, Z-X, y-w, p-b, I-l, and p-q. Joshua did not know the letters *w* and *g*. Possible reasons for these letter confusions might have included visual similarity, position in space (especially with the p-b and p-q), and letter name similarity (U-W).

Further investigation into these assessments revealed that Joshua's greatest difficulty on the Phonemic Awareness assessment was in responding with the correct ending sounds. His response on the Writing Vocabulary assessment was limited; he wrote four words—his first name, his last name, and the words *I* and *a* (*a* was written backward). On the Dictation Task, he demonstrated limited knowledge of letter–sound relationship. He fluctuated between writing the letter for only the beginning sound or only the ending sound to stand for a word, many

	Dictation Task	Letter Identification	Ohio Word Test	Phoneme Awareness	Writing Vocabulary	Oral Reading Analysis
Table 2 Joshua's Assessment Results						
Date						
September						
Raw Score	8/37	45/54	1/20	19/35	4	
Percentage	22%	83%	5%	54%		—
Stanine	1	1	1	—	1	—
December						
Raw Score	34/37	50/54	13/20	34/35	33	Level 2
Percentage	92%	93%	65%	97%		—
Stanine	7	3	6	—	7	—
May						
Raw Score	36/37		18/20		60	Level 9
Percentage	97%	—	90%	—		98%
Stanine	9	—	8	—	9	—

words he did not attempt, and the attempts for a few words had no recognizable letter–sound relationship. He wrote more consonants than vowels. However, he used these letters because he knew he needed to fill space, not because he understood they were consonants. He formed the letters *L* and *a* backward. He also used uppercase letters for *b*, *d*, and *l*. The one word he identified on the Ohio Word Test was *am*. He did attempt two other words, saying the correct beginning letter sound—/t/ for *the* and /h/ for *has*.

I gained helpful insights from the results of the Print Knowledge Task, CVC Word Test, Rhyming Pairs, and Predictable Language Text Retelling Analysis. Joshua's responses to all these tasks were always brief and without elaboration. He confused letter sounds or did not know them. Rhyming proved to be Joshua's strength; he was able to successfully identify some rhyming pairs.

Joshua's greatest difficulty was with the retelling task. For this task, we used the story *The Bus Ride* (McLean, 1993). It is a simple story about a boy, a girl, and a variety of animals boarding a bus at individual stops. The last creature to board the bus is a bee with a very large stinger. After the bee boards the bus, all the characters run off the bus in the order opposite that they entered. Responses to this assessment required for organized thoughts to be expressed orally, something I already had noted as an area of difficulty for Joshua. The retelling analysis showed us that Joshua needed guidance in organizing his thoughts and prompting when retelling a story. Joshua's limited free retelling yielded only 5 out of the 10 characters in no specific order. He also included 1 of the characters twice and added a character that was not a part of this story. He only included one event from the story but used an incorrect verb tense: "All runned out." However, he did not connect this event to any particular problem or solution. In the probed retelling, Joshua was unable to add any more characters. He did, however, shed more light on the problem in the story, saying, "The bumble bee was on it [the bus]. They were going to sting the animals." When asked about the solution, he added only the simple one-word response *run*.

The gloominess of these scores was brightened by Joshua's response to a question I always asked during my initial interview in an attempt to begin meaningful conversation—a point of action—with a student: "What is your favorite thing to do at school?"

"Read!" replied Joshua emphatically. It was heartening that, while many other beginning LEAP students often replied, "Play" or "Recess," Joshua's response was actually in line with the purpose of LEAP.

Of the 51 first-grade students given the full battery of initial assessments, Joshua ranked 22 on our list of perceived greatest needs. Another LEAP teacher and I split the group according to greatest needs, class assignments, and schedules. Joshua ranked 11th in terms of greatest perceived needs out of my initial group of 20 students.

A review of all the assessments helped me begin to plan pertinent instruction geared to meet Joshua's needs. I was aware that Joshua's strengths were in the area of rudimentary sound–symbol relationships and the identification and production of rhyming patterns. Perhaps this was due to a strong emphasis on phonics in our kindergarten program. On the other hand, Joshua had unusual difficulty retelling a story he had heard, which could have been due to limited experiences with print.

I decided to begin instruction with his strengths, to build confidence, and to provide more observation of his word identification skills. This instruction would focus on sound–symbol relationships and move Joshua toward blending practice.

Reflection Point 3.2

Based on Joshua's assessments, what are three strengths you could build on if you were to begin working with him? Write a goal for the initial lesson.

Providing Consistent Support

As mentioned in chapter 2, it is crucial to have classroom teachers and parents consistently supporting reading and using the strategies and materials we know will help children become readers.

LEAP teachers work with their students to bridge the gap between where the students are and where we need to get them. In order to be sure we are consistent with the classroom teachers, we communicate regularly with them regarding students' challenges, successes, and behaviors, and any other concerns or changes. Part of the RIA's lesson with the students relates to the stories from their classroom anthologies using picture walks, choral readings, and comprehension activities. We also review the class spelling words, analyze them, and sort them for similarities. We choose several high-usage words to add to our word wall. Much of the sharing between the classroom teachers and the LEAP team goes on at lunchtime or before and after school in informal conversations.

Before report card time, I provide the classroom teachers with a nine-week assessment summary and a table of scores, including previous scores for each LEAP student, so the teacher can see a snapshot of growth for each student. In Joshua's case, his classroom teacher and I discussed this information and together shared it with Joshua's mother during parent–teacher conferences.

In order to provide consistency at home, after each one-to-one lesson my students take home a folder that has two pages in it: The Parent Expectation Note (see Figure 7) highlights the expectations of follow-through at home, and the Progress Note (see Figure 8) shares areas we worked on in LEAP sessions during the past week. The Progress Note has a place for me to provide specific comments and a place for parents to write back to me. I require a parent's signature on it to indicate he or she has read the information. Joshua's mother often shared a message with me. The comments included a simple "Thank you," questions such as "Should we be reading more?" and the apology "I'm sorry this is late." Sometimes it was a more involved response regarding tutoring or spelling. I was pleased that Joshua's mother took the time to respond.

I also share with parents information sheets about activities to do at home to encourage and raise a successful reader. Periodically, I send home suggestions that encourage talking; listening; language play; vocabulary development; before, during, and after reading activities; and book titles and suggestions for library trips. In addition, every month students take home packets that include a collection of teacher-made books, large-print poems, a current word wall list, a book of blank pages for writing whatever they want, a newsletter written by our district literacy director, and a Sun Valley LEAP news bulletin. Both of the latter have information for promoting family literacy activities.

At every opportunity, I strongly encourage parents to spend time reading with children and discussing what they read with them. As simple as this suggestion seems, it sometimes appears this is a difficult thing for parents to do regularly. Perhaps this is because it requires acquiring a habit that might not already be present, and developing new habits takes energy and requires time. In addition, results from reading to and discussing the reading experience with children are not always evident immediately. Any reading teacher knows, however, that these experiences add up and are a gift to any child for acquiring oral language, developing meaning and vocabulary, building comprehension skills, and creating background knowledge.

To further encourage parent participation and to support the program, students choose an extra book to take home in pouches, in addition to their current leveled books for independent reading. Many

Figure 7
Parent Expectation Note

Dear _____,

I am so glad that you consider learning to read and write important for your child! Here is how you can help _____ tonight.

- Ask your child about the things he or she did at school today.
- Have your child share the booklet or book he or she brought home from school today. Be sure to return it tomorrow.
- Have your child build a sentence from the word cards in the envelope. (The sentence your child should make is the one on the envelope.) Please keep the words and save them in the box we have sent home for them.
- Have a fun review of the words you have been saving in the box. Here are some things you might try. Spread out all the cards or sort them by alphabetical order and spread out. Then ask your child to do several of these activities daily. Find and say the following:
    action words (*like, went, watched, made,* etc.),
    pronouns (words that stand for names: *he, she, it,* etc.),
    describing words (*big, red, happy,* etc.),
    words that begin with *b* (or any other letter of the alphabet),
    words that end with *ing,*
    a word that means the opposite of a word you give (*big/little*), or
    a word that means almost the same as a word you give (*happy/glad*).
- Use these activities every day to help your child recognize, understand, and use these words. Change which questions you use daily. Perhaps you and your child can come up with some of your own word categories, too.
- Read a story to your child and talk about it.
- Make these tasks a positive experience for your child.

By doing these few things on a regular basis with your child, you will be helping him or her grow in his or her own literacy skills.

Sincerely,
Mrs. Wesley
Literacy Intervention Teacher
Sun Valley Elementary School

Figure 8
Progress Note

Dear _____,

This is a note to let you know what we have been doing in LEAP this week. Ask _____ about the areas checked below to get even more information. Please return the bottom of the sheet to me. Thanks for your response.

___ reading new stories   ___ retelling stories

___ rereading stories   ___ writing sentences

___ figuring out new words   ___ making stories

___ making words   ___ spelling words

___ listening to stories

Sincerely,
Mrs. Wesley
Literacy Intervention Teacher
Sun Valley Elementary School

****************RETURN THE BOTTOM PART TOMORROW! Thanks!****************

Dear Mrs. Wesley,

Thanks for the information on what my child is learning. I wanted to let you know

_____

_____

_____

_____

_____
(signed)

_____
(date)

students are excited about the opportunity to take these books home. These extra books might include an individual copy of a story in the classroom anthology so the parents and children can share the classroom story experience; a commercial beginning-to-read book so parents can see what is available at the library or bookstore; a classic fairy tale, poem, or nursery rhyme book; or a nonfiction book of interest to the children. I include a Read to Me bookmark in each book, indicating that this is a book to be read *to* the child not *by* the child. When students are new to the program, I also include a brief note explaining to parents the purpose of the extra books. Because many families do not have books at home, these books provide appropriate extra reading material. I also continue to encourage parents to visit the public library to check out other books.

Joshua's mother asked for books from the LEAP library. She also bought a few audio books for the boys to listen to at home. However, as the year went by, it seemed that most of the family's homework time was spent on spelling. She even shared that they were caught up in spelling and had little time for reading. Being prepared for the spelling test was important for Joshua's mother. She delighted in his improved spelling test scores. Nothing was wrong with this, but it seemed that this task was always given preference, perhaps to the exclusion of time spent reading and talking about what was read. This became a frustrating issue for me because this kind of unbalanced focus weakens consistency of the support students deserve.

However, Joshua's mother did ask me to send home more books, and I was happy to do so. During the second semester I also sent home frog bookbags. Each drawstring bag, made from bright frog-print material, contained a book for parents to read to their child as well as materials and instructions for an interactive activity such as making a puppet. The five bags rotated among students. Each student took the bag for two nights at home, just in case the family had a busy night already planned for the first night a frog bookbag came home.

Joshua was excited when it was his turn to take one of the five bags home. However, several days after its expected return to school, it still had not appeared. The next time I saw Joshua, I asked him about the bookbag.

Kathleen: Where is the frog bookbag?

Joshua: I haven't done it.

Kathleen: Any reason why, Joshua?

Joshua: All my mom does is cook and talk on the phone. She won't read it to me.

Of course, Joshua's mother had other responsibilities and perhaps Joshua had not communicated the purpose of the bag to his parents or his grandmother, who watched him frequently. Joshua's frog bookbag did finally appear—although it was many days late—and he had completed the activity.

Reflection Point 3.3

To help families balance their activities and responsibilities to prioritize and provide times for reading and writing, create a flier or calendar offering suggestions. Consider providing parents with a list of local resources, such as events at a local library or bookstore.

Family Literacy Nights

Another way we addressed consistent support at home was through Family Literacy Nights. Our first Family Literacy Night was similar to an open house. I greeted the families and gave an overview of the LEAP program. I told parents about the power they invoke when they follow through sharing with their child that reading and writing are important in their homes. I shared my reading philosophy with the families and enlisted their support.

I also shared with parents the reading development they might expect to see their children experience during the year. I demonstrated focal points from a general LEAP lesson to show how we direct learning for the children and move them toward reading competency.

I emphasized listening to the child read at home and reading to the child. I modeled activities that would be sent home in pouches. I shared this information with parents so students would receive consistent support at home.

I encouraged parents to ask questions and engage in conversation with me. For example, some of comments included the following:

- Yes, it will sound like your child has memorized the book or is just reading the pictures at first. That's OK; children who are early readers went through this step, too. It's an important part of becoming a reader.

- No, don't cover the pictures. We do teach the students to refer to the pictures as one source of information or verification for unknown words. Other strategies are asking What letter does the word begin with? Does it make sense? Or, you can direct your child to reread the sentences to help figure out the right word.

I also had a special sheet at the sign-in table where parents could indicate if they wanted me to call them regarding their child because Family Literacy Nights are not about individual conferencing.

I usually have door prizes for those families who attend Family Literacy Night. The prizes are inexpensive and related to encouraging family time with reading and writing. The prizes have included the following:

- spiral notebooks
- frog pencils
- inexpensive books
- colored marker pens
- children's stationery

When I present a prize, I demonstrate how to use it in a meaningful way to support reading and writing at home. For example, a spiral notebook could serve as a journal. The student might write his or her own sentence for each day of vacation and include an illustration. He or she also might use it for making plans for a birthday party or a holiday gift list.

Joshua's mother attended our first Family Literacy Night. I was especially pleased because she had already had a child participate in our LEAP program. In similar situations a parent might choose not to come, figuring he or she already knows what I am going to say. To me, Joshua's mother's presence signaled a positive interest in her son's education. Also, I never present my information in exactly the same manner, so a second exposure to this information might be seen or heard by parents in a valuable way.

Reflection Point 3.4

Create a list of activities you would suggest to encourage reading and writing at home. Share your list with several grade-level colleagues to compare ideas. How could you share these ideas most effectively with parents?

Read Across America

In addition to Family Literacy Night, in March, with the help of Student Council, we have another family evening for all primary-grade students and their families. The focal point is Read Across America—a national celebration of Dr. Seuss's birthday that focuses on reading to children. All of our activities demonstrate to families the ways in which they can interact with their children to build on the reading processes and to incorporate reading and writing into their lives on a daily basis.

Our Read Across America evening began with the entire group meeting in the cafetorium. The school principal and I both spoke to the purposes and the significance of family involvement through reading at home. Next, we divided the group by markings placed beforehand on each family's program for the evening. We began rotating the families through the four events hosted by teacher volunteers. Student Council members assisted the teachers as well as greeted families and directed traffic through the halls. Some of our events were the following:

Fun With Words: Friendly competitions among families showed how many words could be made from the letters in the phrase *Read*

Across America. In a separate activity, I demonstrated how families could have fun with various word-sort activities.

Dr. Seuss Writing: Families let rhymes roll off their tongues and onto the paper in Dr. Seuss fashion. They shared their writing with others in the group.

Guest Readers: Parent and community volunteers read from favorite books in the library.

Parent Interviews: Students interviewed their parents with a pretend microphone, inquiring about what school was like for them and what their favorite stories were when they were their children's ages.

Flashlight Reading: Families read favorite books by flashlight in a darkened room.

At the end of the rotations, everyone returned to the cafetorium for concluding remarks and free books. Each child who attended took home a book that had been purchased by Student Council.

The year that Joshua was in my LEAP group, the evening was a success, with over 200 parents and children attending. I was delighted to see Joshua, his brother, and his mother attend and participate in our activities.

Trip to the Library

During the last weeks of school, I held a parent–child get-together one evening at the public library in order to promote the library's summer reading program. The program offered an opportunity to extend students' reading over the summer months.

My turnout at this event was not large—Joshua's family did not attend this event—but the time spent was not in vain. For several families it was their first visit to the library. Their children left with a desire to return, the parents had an idea of how the library system works, and everyone had their own library cards. The students were very proud of this new possession.

Planning Pertinent Instruction

While we waited for all parents to return permission forms so their children could participate in LEAP, the RIA, Mrs. Martin, and I organized and conducted exploration sessions for our prospective students. Our goal was to observe how each student interacted with print materials. I modeled each activity, and Mrs. Martin observed the enthusiastic students. These activities, described below, helped us plan for pertinent instruction.

ABC Practice includes a large alphabet chart and a special pointer, a Chinese back scratcher, for students to use when pointing to each letter as they read or sing the alphabet. ABC Practice allows teachers to make observations regarding one-to-one correspondence, knowledge of the alphabet, and unusual confusions (for example, one student once said "l-m-n-o-p" for just one letter).

ABC Puzzles allow students to select and organize letters in alphabetical order. We observed that students often asked for this activity first, perhaps because of their familiarity with the puzzle format or the fact that there was only one possible way to complete the activity.

Book Tubs offer a collection of alphabet books and familiar favorites for students to explore. While interacting with a chosen book, students demonstrate their print knowledge, interest in printed material, and level of involvement.

Letter Matching involves students in pairing uppercase and lowercase magnetic letters. An alphabet chart is available as a model, if needed. Many children referenced the chart, while others could not locate specific letters on the chart.

Letter–Sound Matching uses a collection of small plastic objects that includes animals, balls, and little erasers. The students identify each object, listen for its beginning sound, and then place the item above its corresponding letter on the alphabet strip—a border with the alphabet and pictures of a corresponding item that begins with each letter of the alphabet.

Students quickly engaged in this activity. The students loved to touch and name the objects, listen for the beginning sounds, search for the letters on the alphabet strip, and then place the objects in the correct places. The alphabet strip offered the support of alphabetical order if students were familiar with the concept; however, many students were not yet familiar with where to find a needed letter quickly or did not even know what letter they should be looking for.

Letter Tile Sort allows students to combine letters to make words they know, to select and organize the tiles in alphabetical order, or to simply sort letters into groups of like letters. The teacher is able to see the choices each child makes in his or her play with the tiles.

Writing Practice encourages the students to write as many words or letters as they can on white boards. Mrs. Martin and I made observations regarding students' grasp of word or letter knowledge, sound–symbol relationships, sound sequence, letter formation, and students' ability to read what they wrote. Most students, including Joshua, could not write many words on their own, but they experimented by using the markers to make letters, write an occasional original word, or copy a word from somewhere in the room.

All these activities are nonthreatening and engaging. Our small group size invited more opportunities for meaningful conversations about the activities and attention for each student than a whole-class setting. Joshua and the other students were excited when allowed to explore and rotate through these activities.

Reflection Point 3.5

Once you have planned such exploration activities, how would you record your observations to have this information in a useful format for planning pertinent instruction? Create your own record sheet. How does your record sheet lend itself for individual, small-group, or whole-class instructional planning?

Our First One-to-One Lesson

Joshua's and my first one-to-one lesson included using magnetic letters on a cookie sheet to allow for his easy exploration of letter combinations and words. We used the word *am* to begin our magnetic letter experience and quickly moved to making rhyming pattern words using the chunks *-at* and *-an*. This activity utilized Joshua's existing strength with rhyming words to introduce him to letter sounds he had not yet mastered. It also gave Joshua practice blending sounds to make words. In this activity, I began by manipulating letters on a cookie sheet between us.

Kathleen: Joshua, here is the word *at*. Let's see if we can add a letter and make a new word. What letter is this?

Joshua: *C.*

Kathleen: What sounds can it make?

Joshua: /k/, /s/.

Kathleen: Let's try that first sound and add it to the other sounds we already have. What new word can we make?

Joshua: /c/, /a/, /t/...*cat*!

After making several words such as *cat, hat, mat, fat,* and *bat,* I left the *-at* chunk in the middle of the cookie sheet and assembled the remaining selected initial consonants across the top of the tray. This time I said, "hat," and Joshua selected the correct letter, added it to the *-at* chunk, then pulled the magnetic letters down to the bottom of the cookie sheet, saying the letter sounds as he did. Finally, Joshua blended the sounds to say the word. We continued this process with *-an* chunks.

Joshua and other students often had difficulty with directionality, that is, getting their letters or sounds in the correct left-to-right order. To support these students I use a small sticker, sometimes an orange dot or a tiny green frog, to indicate where to begin. During this activity, I encouraged Joshua to use his pointer finger to sweep from left to right, beginning at the sticker and sounding each letter in the correct order.

Joshua and I moved to a sorting activity using cards with *-at* and *-an* rimes.

Kathleen:	Joshua, let's read these words and see if they have anything in common.
Joshua:	*Mat, bat.*
Kathleen:	Hmm...do you notice anything the same about them?
Joshua:	Mat, bat... [He points to the *t*s.]
Kathleen:	I think I see more. Tell me what else you see.
Joshua:	Oh, they both have *a* and *t*!
Kathleen:	That's right! They do! Let's group them together. Now let's pick another word and read that word.
Joshua:	M-a-n...*man.*
Kathleen:	Could we group *man* with *mat* and *bat*? What do you think, Joshua? Or should we set it aside to see if we can find words to go with it and make a new group?
Joshua:	No. It doesn't have *-at.* [He sets it aside and pulls another card from the small pile of words.] F-a-n...*fan.* It goes with *man.*
Kathleen:	Can you tell me why?
Joshua:	They both have *n.*
Kathleen:	Do they have anything else the same?
Joshua:	Oh, they both have *-an.*

Joshua continued to sound out words, read them, and sort them by their ending chunks. I followed this activity by asking Joshua to locate specific words within our word sort. All of these activities required Joshua to concentrate on the similarities and differences in words as well as attend to sound sequence within a word—all pertinent instruction planned to meet Joshua's needs.

Joshua's Progression Through Reading Levels

My experience with students in LEAP has led me to conclude that patterns in growth of reading relate generally to book levels. Because of the book characteristics—such as sentence length, patterns, and return sweep—at each level, students seem to need to spend more time at some levels. My theory is that once students master the characteristics of level 3 books, they seem to be able to quickly progress through the levels until they come to level 6. I have found that this level again often requires more time before a student moves on to the next levels. The same pattern repeats at level 10. I have organized the remainder of this chapter to reflect the ebb and flow of Joshua's reading growth through the numbered levels.

Joshua's early reading experience began with a level 1 book. Books in levels 1 and 2 contain characteristics such as strong picture clues, limited words, and few lines per page. These characteristics proved valuable as Joshua developed understandings of voice–print match, directionality, return sweep, and other print knowledge skills.

For our first lesson, we used a level 1 book, *Dressing Up* (Randell, Giles, & Smith, 1996b), which features photographs of young children dressed as different animals or characters. The repetitive text supports the beginning reader. We began with a picture walk.

> **Kathleen:** Have you ever dressed up and pretended to be an animal or a special character?
>
> [Joshua shakes his head slightly.]
>
> **Kathleen:** In this book the children are dressed up in costumes. Let's see what they are pretending to be....

After the picture walk, our goal was to match voice to print, being aware that the space between words shows where one word stops and another word begins. We paid special attention to the beginning sounds of each word.

> **Kathleen:** What is the first word on this page? Put your finger under the first sound in that word.

This instruction anchored Joshua to match his voice with the print. We then proceeded to the teaching point of cross-checking the beginning sound of a word with the picture.

> **Kathleen:** Do you have your finger under the first sound? OK, get your mouth ready to say that sound. Now check the

picture. Is that still the sound you want to use? Does it look right? Will the word sound right? Then ask your brain...does it make sense?

I purposely chose a book I thought would guarantee high success. I had already learned that Joshua was a bit shy or apprehensive about stepping out into uncharted territories. My primary purpose was to build a safe foundation from which we could move forth to fortify his developing skills and lead him to increase his willingness to take risks. Joshua followed my prompts and accurately read *Dressing Up*.

Reflection Point 3.6

Have you ever worked with a child like Joshua who requires much assurance? Discuss with a colleague what worked effectively to support that student. Generate a list of activities to help increase a student's risk-taking abilities.

Joshua's Draft Book Work

After our successful work with *Dressing Up*, I asked Joshua to write a related sentence in his draft book and prompted him to think about a costume in the book that he might like to try. Those thoughts evolved into his intended sentence: I am a dinosaur. Joshua wrote the following: *I o m a.*

We discussed the difference between letters and words, and Joshua changed *o m* to *am*. He had to check our alphabet sheet to see how the letter *a* was formed. I covered his first writing with correction tape ("magic tape") and he rewrote the word correctly on the fresh space. However, he was still stuck on the word *dinosaur*.

Kathleen: Joshua, haven't you seen that word recently? Do you think you could find it again? Where could you start? Where could you look for that word?

[Joshua pauses.]

Kathleen: Let's look at the book!

[We thumb through the pages and stop when we find the page with the dinosaur picture.]

Kathleen: Maybe it's on this page. Joshua, would you read this page to me?

Joshua: "I am a dinosaur."

Kathleen: Which word do you think is *dinosaur*?

[Joshua points to the correct word.]

Kathleen: That's right! How did you know that word was *dinosaur*?

[Joshua smiles as he continues to point to the word *dinosaur*.]

Kathleen: Tell me Joshua, how did you figure out that word was *dinosaur*?

[Joshua continues to smile but says nothing.]

Kathleen: Oh, did you hear that /d/ sound and see the big word that begins with *d*? *Dinosaur* is a big word, isn't it?

[Joshua nods.]

Kathleen: Let's read that sentence again.

[Joshua and Kathleen read together: "I am a dinosaur."]

Kathleen: Yes, that is where the word *dinosaur* would be.

[Joshua affirms this conclusion by nodding his head.]

We decided it was OK to use the word in the book as a resource for our writing. Joshua appeared glad to have a solution to his dilemma and correctly wrote the word *dinosaur* in his draft book. Then, I rewrote the sentence onto a sentence strip as Joshua read it to me. I cut the sentence strip into individual words and scrambled them. Then, I asked Joshua to recreate the sentence and read it back to me. (See Figure 9 for cut-up sentence activities.) He successfully ordered the words. We went on to "play" with the words. I had him locate specific words and then locate words that began with a particular letter or sound. He was successful with all of these activities. I had planned pertinent instruction so that the lesson would allow for success and teach Joshua how he

---

Figure 9
Cut-Up Sentence Activities

Before Cutting Up Sentence

Reread the sentence to see if I wrote it correctly.

Here's a marker. Underline all the vowels (or consonant letter combinations) you see.

After Cutting Up Sentence Into Individual Words

I just mixed up your sentence. Put it back together.

Which word is the beginning of the sentence? How did you know?

Which word is the end of the sentence? How did you know?

Find a word that begins with _____.

Find all the words that begin with _____.

Find a word that ends with _____.

Find a word that rhymes with _____.

Find a word that has this sound in the middle: _____.

Hide your eyes and I will take away a word. What word is missing?

Make a new sentence with some of or all of these words.

Sorting

Find words that have the same chunks.

Find some words that are action words.

Find some words that are naming words.

Find some words that have something in common such as rhyme or two-letter phonograms.

Generated by Literacy Intervention Teachers in the Peoria Unified School District, Peoria, Arizona, USA

---

could problem solve for himself. It wasn't that he couldn't do it; he just hadn't learned how to do it.

Identifying and Dealing With Communication Problems

While observing Joshua's interactions in the LEAP classroom over the next few weeks, I became acutely aware of his limited verbal responses. He seldom took initiative in conversing with Mrs. Martin or me. Conversation appeared painful and somewhat unnatural for him as if he were unsure of what to say or how to respond. I often wondered,

Did he understand me? Was he afraid to answer for fear his answer might not be correct? Was he trying to organize information for a response? Was he searching for the right word to fit what he wanted to say? Was he trying to put words into a complete sentence? Was he waiting for someone to supply the answer?

Reflection Point 3.7 _____

Think for a moment about students who you know who give limited verbal responses. Does the difficulty lie in receptive language (i.e., taking in verbal information) or expressive language (i.e., organizing thoughts to share verbally with others)? What leads you to that conclusion? List several things that you might do to encourage oral language development. Speech and language teachers are great sources of ideas.

_____

As Mrs. Martin and I planned pertinent instruction to support Joshua's growth in communication and confidence, we set general expectations. I began by sharing with Joshua that when I engaged in conversation with others, I enjoyed having eye contact with them. I demonstrated what this meant. Then, Joshua and I practiced making eye contact while using very quick verbal exchanges.

Kathleen: My eyes like to see your eyes when I talk to you. Did you enjoy reading your book?

Joshua: Yes.

Kathleen: Tell me what you did last night.

Joshua: Church, bed.

[Joshua answers but does not maintain eye contact.]

Kathleen: Remember, whenever we talk, my eyes like to see your eyes.

Next, we discussed different kinds of responses to questions. Yes, there could be shrugs, nods, and one-word answers. However, responding with complete sentences would be much more desirable. We had many conversations around the attributes of a complete sentence, and I created opportunities for Joshua to practice responding in complete sentences. I let Joshua know that Mrs. Martin and I expected him to reply to us in this manner. This consistent support was necessary for his growth.

Not every engagement with Joshua resulted in appropriate eye contact and use of complete sentences. However, the expectations were set, modeled, practiced, and reinforced consistently throughout the year. Even with all this attention, Joshua did not become the most fluent conversationalist. I discussed my concerns with his mother and let her know what I was doing with and expecting from Joshua. His mother appeared to understand yet registered no real response when I shared this information with her.

Later in the year, Joshua's classroom teacher and I contacted his mother about referring Joshua for a speech and language development screening. At this point, his mother wanted to know more. Earlier she had seemed to understand, but now the matter seemed more pressing, perhaps because she feared a special education label. I explained to Joshua's mother that teachers of language processing and speech articulation are specially trained to diagnose difficulties in these areas and design instruction and practice for each child. With his mother's permission, I referred Joshua for the appropriate screening. Although the speech teacher noted some areas of need such as syntax and vocabulary usage, Joshua did not qualify for special assistance.

Without this added support, I sought to build Joshua's language development applying my own knowledge and experience, developing plans, and using them to the best of my ability. I observed that engaging Joshua in conversation after long absences, particularly winter and spring breaks, was like starting all over again—which, of course, we did. Again, I set expectations, demonstrated models, and provided Joshua with practice opportunities.

The tone of two of his most frequent responses led me to further conclusions: Joshua lacked the confidence, courage, and initiative to experiment with new strategies. When I would make suggestions about things to try, such as a particular strategy to apply to figure out an unknown word, he might respond with "I can?" Joshua always said these words with the inflection of a question rather than the emphatic "I can!" from the I-think-I-can attitude I encouraged. For example, once when he was explaining that he didn't have anyone to read to the night before, I suggested that he could read to his grandmother, who often baby-sat him before his mother came home from work. He immediately responded, "I can?" as though the idea had never occurred to him.

"Ask her and see what she thinks," I replied. "She might really enjoy hearing you read, and that will give Mom a little time to start dinner." Again, he looked at me as though I had just unlocked a door to something totally new.

His other frequent response was "It is?" said with the same inflection of uncertainty. He often gave this response following my acknowledgment of his attempts to answer puzzling questions. He then proceeded with a brave attempt at the answer again. He also did this when I pinpointed and reinforced his correct use of a strategy to solve an unknown word.

In general, Joshua didn't appear to have confidence in his own abilities. He was hesitant to venture forth with options available to him, to apply information, to make decisions, or even to acknowledge his own successes. Joshua was just beginning to discover that he had power over situations, that he could make different choices and achieve different results. I was hoping that this knowledge would be the beginning of some big changes in his outlook, and I was prepared to use our time together to encourage his recently awakened powers.

I knew I had to lay a safe and secure foundation from which Joshua would explore reading strategies. We needed to establish the kind of mutual trust that Debbie Miller writes about in *Reading With Meaning: Teaching Comprehension in the Primary Grades* (2002). Joshua also needed opportunities to think about his options, to select alternatives, to try different strategies, and to learn that his first choice might not necessarily work. He needed to know that he didn't have to be right from the beginning. If one strategy didn't work, he had choices. He could go back to other possibilities, try a logical path, and then evaluate again. There was no need to just stay stuck.

Reflection Point 3.8

Reflect on experiences in your life when you exercised persistence or demonstrated resilience. Think about children you have taught and their experiences or lack of experiences with persistence and resilience. With a colleague, discuss why persistence and resilience are important life skills. How can the points of action help develop or nurture these skills?

Level 2

During his first few months in LEAP, Joshua showed little gain through the Reading Recovery–leveled books we used. In December, he was still reading at level 2, yet we had made substantial gains in many of the areas that are prerequisite for moving more rapidly through the leveled books (refer to Table 2 on page 56). It was clear Joshua was acquiring skills but not applying them consistently.

Joshua's success in phonemic awareness increased through the word-study segment of our lesson plan. His accuracy on blending in the Stahl and Murray Phonemic Segmentation Task rose from 67% to 100%. His score for identification of beginning and ending sounds in isolation went from 45% to 95%, a gain of 50 percentage points (Table 2 does not reflect individual blending and isolation scores). He scored at perfect and near-perfect levels at this task. I attributed this achievement to reading and rereading books and a variety of experiences in word building. We practiced breaking and making words with our magnetic letters, really listening to where we heard the sound, and then blending the sounds together. We also had speed contests to develop fluency. We sorted words by their similar patterns and then reread our sorts to develop fluency.

In one small-group activity with Mrs. Martin, Joshua and the other boys practiced changing vowel sounds in the word *bug*. Mrs. Martin wrote the consonants on a ladybug cutout, and a piece of paper served as a slide that moved through the ladybug to change the vowels. Each time the boys viewed a new word: *bug, bag, beg, big, bog*. The group learned about the flexibility of the English language; they learned that a new word can be created by keeping the beginning and ending consonant of a word intact and changing the vowel.

The group also participated in a variety of lessons involving making words. In one lesson, they followed Mrs. Martin's directions, making two-, three-, and four-letter words and then larger words until they made a mystery word: *pumpkins*.

Pumpkins

up	pin	skin	pumpkin	pumpkins
us	ink	sink		
is	kin	spin		
	sun	pink		
		sunk		
		pump		

Joshua's ability to write sounds in words on the dictation task sentences reflected this practice; he was now scoring at a stanine 7, well above average. Joshua represented 34 out of 37 possible sounds.

Our sentence writing still concentrated on teaching ways to deal with difficulties Joshua encountered in directionality. He always slowed down a bit when he came to the letters *p*, *d*, *b*, *g*, or *q* because he often confused these letters. His confusion was not surprising. Because of their spatial positioning, these letters are more difficult to learn for many children. Finding this an opportunity for pertinent instruction, I said, "Joshua, let's stop for a minute. Is this a letter we need to have a little extra time to think about? Where can we look to double-check on how we make this letter?"

"The word wall?" Joshua replied. Or, another time Joshua replied, "The alphabet chart?" He still was cautious in his replies, rather than confident. However, these were signs that he was beginning to develop some confidence; Joshua now ventured reasonable attempts to answer questions.

Joshua also often confused the order of letters when writing two-letter words such as *is* and *in*. So, I used the magnetic letters to manipulate and demonstrate letter order on the cookie sheet. Joshua listened to the first sound and placed the first sound next to the orange dot, which told us where to begin. Then, he placed the second sound next to the first sound. Next, he pulled each letter down a few inches, saying the sounds as he did. Finally, he blended the sounds to read the two-letter word. I used this same method when Joshua confused the letter order when writing *hs* instead of *sh* in words such as *she* or *shop*. After I manipulated magnets to show letter order correctly, I asked Joshua to write these words on our white board. Joshua, and other LEAP students, enjoyed using colored markers on the white board, and this activity brought us back to our original objective of writing sounds and letters in the correct order.

Word order occasionally presented difficulty for Joshua, too. Therefore, we planned pertinent instruction using cut-up sentences. I always asked Joshua to reassemble the words in the original order in which we had written the sentence. Sometimes when he reassembled his cut-up sentences, Joshua used all the words but the syntax was out of order. Therefore, I directed him to reread the sentence.

Joshua: "The animals for dinner came."

[Joshua pauses.]

Kathleen: Does that make sense?

Joshua: No.

Kathleen: I wonder if we could rearrange some of the words?

After several rearrangements, Joshua had a sentence that made sense when he read it.

Joshua: "The animals came for dinner!"

Another difficulty Joshua faced was following directions. He often had lengthy delays when trying to follow directions, so we concentrated on trying to remember them. I tried to give him a visual picture with the prompt "Hold on to those directions." If he had lengthy delays in his responses, I might prompt him by asking, "What is it you are trying to do?" If the task was listening for ending sounds, he was expected to reply, "I'm listening for ending sounds." This procedure allowed him to slow down, think back, remember—or "grab hold of"—the original directions, and begin to refocus on the designated task, a minilesson in metacognition. All my prompts helped Joshua clarify his purpose.

The picture walks we did before reading a new book provided opportunities for Joshua to practice other areas of need: vocabulary development, expressive language, and correct verb tenses. For example, the following picture walk took place when I introduced the book *Stop!* (Randell, 1996h).

Kathleen: Joshua, here is our new book. What do you think the children on the front of this book are doing?

Joshua: Looking?

Kathleen: I wonder what they are looking for? They seem to be near a street. What do you think?

Joshua: Cars?

Kathleen: Maybe; I wonder why they would be looking for cars?

Joshua: They want to cross the street.

Kathleen: Oh, why would they want to look for cars if they are going to cross the street?

Joshua: So, they don't get runned over.

Kathleen: Oh, so they don't get run over. If that were so, Joshua, what would you tell these kids to do before they cross the street?

Joshua: Stop. Look for cars.

Kathleen: What should they do if they see a car?

Joshua: Stay there.

Kathleen: Great! Another word we might use if a car is coming would be *wait*. The children should wait if they see a car coming. Are there other things the children should watch for before they cross the street, Joshua? Let's take a look at more of the book and find out.

As we continued our picture walk through the book we found that there were other things the children should wait for, such as motorcycles, trucks, and bikes.

Kathleen: Joshua, when can the kids cross the street?

Joshua: When nothing is coming down the street anymore.

Through meaningful conversation about the pictures in a new story, I continually demonstrated and engaged Joshua in the process of making connections, constructing meaning, naming objects, using correct verb tenses, and preparing to read the story.

In December, Joshua still wasn't attending to print to the degree necessary to become a good reader. I encouraged him to be exact in placing his finger under the first sound of the word so that his finger would show his eyes where to look, and to get his mouth ready to say the word. This strategy proved to be especially helpful when reading *Cat and Mouse* (Randell, 1996c). In this story, Joshua continually appeared to get caught up in the pattern of the story but neglected to keep pace with the change of the pattern—sometimes the cat and mouse went over objects in their chase and sometimes they went under objects.

This story offered not only good practice for the attention-to-print strategies mentioned above but also an opportunity to practice cross-checking. I modeled these strategies for Joshua:

Kathleen: My finger is under the beginning sound. This helps my eyes know what to read. My mouth gets ready to say the first sound /o/. I quickly check the picture. Yes, the mouse is going over the boxes. *Over* begins with *o*. That looks right, sounds right, and it makes sense.

I continued to slow down Joshua's reading to practice these strategies.

Reflection Point 3.9

If you are familiar with how to administer an Oral Reading Analysis or running record, select a student and a story that you feel is at instructional level for that student. Use paper and pencil to record the student's reading of the story. Analyze your recording, and share with a colleague what you have learned about the student's interaction with print. If you are not familiar with Oral Reading Analysis or running records, this would be a valuable area for further investigation (see Box 3.1 for resources on assessments).

After he reread the story with higher accuracy, I asked Joshua to tell me everything he could remember about the story. I decided to use question words to prompt his retelling of the whole story.

Joshua: Cat tried to catch him.

Kathleen: Who?

Joshua: The mouse, but he didn't catch him.

Kathleen: Why?

Joshua: He, the mouse was running too fast.

Kathleen: Why? Tell me more?

Joshua: He didn't want to get eaten?

Kathleen: Where did the mouse go? How did he get away?

Joshua: He went under the door.

Box 3.1
Resources on Assessments

Clay, M.M. (1993). *An observation survey of early literacy achievement*. Portsmouth, NH: Heinemann.

Fountas, I.C., & Pinnell, G.S. (1996). *Guided reading: Good first teaching for all children*. Portsmouth, NH: Heinemann.

Johnston, P.H. (2000). *Running records: A self-tutoring guide*. Portland, ME: Stenhouse.

Reutzel, D.R., & Cooter, R.B., Jr. (2002). *Strategies for reading assessment and instruction: Helping every child succeed* (2nd ed.). Englewood Cliffs, NJ: Prentice Hall.

Taberski, S. (2000). *On solid ground: Strategies for teaching reading K–3*. Portsmouth, NH: Heinemann.

Joshua had a good understanding of the story, but he still needed to develop the language and format in which to retell the experience. We continued with this work as Joshua moved to level 3.

Levels 3–5

By January, Joshua was ready to move from level 2 to 3. As mentioned before, we had spent an unusually lengthy time on the first two levels. The level 3 books present new text challenges. Some of these challenges include punctuation going on to the next line, an increase in expected sight words, and more words per page. Through my experiences as a LEAP teacher, I found that students who don't make the move from level 2 to level 3 easily often have other learning difficulties. In fact, despite hard work to untangle their reading challenges, many of these students eventually qualify for some sort of special education services because of their challenges. I was concerned about Joshua being able to make the transition.

Joshua and I began level 3 with *The Merry Go Round* (Randell, 1996g). After a picture walk and introduction to the proper names of the children in the story, Joshua began his reading. He was able to read the story at an oral reading instructional level.

I chose two teaching points to offer pertinent instruction. The first was to skip the unknown word, read on, and return to figure out the word using meaning gained from the rest of the sentence plus beginning sounds. The second was to attend to the little words. Joshua substituted *it* for *at, is* for *the, the* for *a,* and *on* for *no.* Again, this had a lot to do with attention-to-print issues and overreliance on oral language patterns. Joshua actually caught himself twice in this area and provided two self-corrections. He also slowed his reading to attend to these matters in his reread. These were true signs that Joshua was beginning to integrate two strategies—monitoring and self-correcting.

To help structure Joshua's retelling of stories I used the following format:

Somebody (a character)

Wants (something)

But (story problem)

So (story solution)

Box 3.2
Resources on Retelling

Benson, V., & Cummins, C. (2000). *The power of retelling: Developmental steps for building comprehension.* New York: Wright Group/McGraw-Hill.

Hansen, J. (2004). *"Tell me a story": Developmentally appropriate retelling strategies.* Newark, DE: International Reading Association.

Hoyt, L. (2000). *Snapshots: Literacy minilessons up close.* Portsmouth, NH: Heinemann.

Morrow, L.M. (2002). *The literacy center: Contexts for reading and writing* (2nd ed.). Portland, ME: Stenhouse.

Morrow, L.M., Gambrell, L.B., & Pressley, M. (Eds.). (2003). *Best practices in literacy instruction* (2nd ed.). New York: Guilford.

Taberski, S. (2000). *On solid ground: Strategies for teaching reading K–3.* Portsmouth, NH: Heinemann.

If Joshua could choose a character to identify with the term *somebody*, then provide answers to the other prompting words from the perspective of that character, he would have a concise, yet complete and accurate, retelling of the story in one sentence (see Box 3.2 for resources on retelling). Joshua still wasn't able to do this task completely on his own. By providing pertinent instruction—that is, modeling and prompting a framework and then using it repeatedly—I hoped that he would eventually be able to use this schema to organize his thoughts to retell stories in a very basic way.

Reflection Point 3.10

Use a tape recorder to record a student's retelling of a story he or she has read. Try using the rating scale in Figure 10 to examine your findings. Is your student strong in retelling? Does he or she require prompting? Is there a specific category of retelling in which your student requires additional instruction? Give an example of a lesson you might use to increase success in this category.

Figure 10
Wesley Rating Scale for Story Analysis

Without Prompting (Tell me about the story.)

Characters	20%
Setting	20%
Problem	20%
Solution	20%
Organization/Sequence	20%

With Incomplete Prompt (Can you tell me more about...?)

Characters

Setting

Problem

Solution

Organization/Sequence

If prompted, the student can obtain no more than half of the remaining points available for each category from the original unprompted analysis.

For example, if a student got 5/10 characters on the unprompted analysis, he or she would get 10%. When later given a prompt, the most he or she could earn for that category would be an additional 5%.

Score the unprompted analysis first. Then score the prompted analysis section and add the two scores together for a total score. Further analysis of the scoring gives a visual breakdown of the student's strengths and needs in story analysis. One can determine if the student is strong in unprompted analysis or if the student relies on prompting, as well as determine which category of the analysis needs further development.

Below is a model of what the scoring might look like.

Without Prompting		**Additional Points With Prompting**	
Characters	15%	Characters	3%
Setting	0%	Setting	5%
Problem	20%	Problem	0%
Solution	20%	Solution	0%
Organization/Sequence	10%	Organization/Sequence	5%
	65%	plus additional 13% = 78%	

Without prompting, this student is strong in problem/solution but challenged in the areas of character, setting, and organization. However, with additional prompting he scored overall in the adequate range.

85%–100% = Great

70%–84% = Adequate

Below 70% = Needs Instruction

We continued to read level 3 books through January. I often high-lighted the same type of teaching points and included a new one—Where have I seen this word before?—because Joshua was having some difficulty remembering a word from one page to the next:

Kathleen: Joshua, have we seen that word before?

Joshua: Yes.

Kathleen: Let's look back and find it.

[Joshua thumbs back a page or two until he finds the word.]

Kathleen: OK, I see you found it. Let's read that old sentence again.

[Joshua reads.]

Kathleen: What was the difficult word?

[Joshua points to the word, then says it.]

Kathleen: Now let's read that word again in the new sentence.

[Joshua reads.]

Kathleen: That's right, now that is something you can do on your own whenever you come to a word you know you've seen before but are having trouble with.

By February, Joshua was ready for level 4. He still made errors similar to the ones described previously, but his rate of self-correcting was beginning to improve. He sometimes made an error using visual information but often returned to self-correct the word using meaning (e.g., *her-here*, *happy-hungry*, *Tom-to*). Joshua was becoming a more independent reader. Structural errors (i.e., *comed* for *came*) continued to slow down his reading, though. I continued to model correct verb tenses and expose him to them.

Joshua moved through two levels—4 and 5—in February. His pace was picking up. My experience told me that if Joshua easily made the next hurdle, moving from level 5 to 6, he would most likely continue smoothly through the next levels as long as he had the consistent support and pertinent instruction.

Later in the spring, Joshua's mother employed a tutor for Joshua and his brother. She complained to me about the cost and the time. However, she also shared the following: "She [the tutor] sets up the tutoring in the public library. Each boy spends 45 minutes with her. Then, guess what? They each get to spend 15 minutes looking for books in the library! Isn't that great?"

You can imagine my frustration. I had been trying to get Joshua's mother to spend time reading books and discussing stories with her son, and now she was paying someone else to get the book selection part started. However, as a teacher, I have learned over the years that some things I perceive as simple are not received as such. Maybe the seeds I had planted concerning self-selected reading had taken root so that she was more receptive to the tutor's actions. Therefore, I delighted in the fact that the boys would have more time with books and perhaps this would help lead them to use the library more often. I continued planning Family Literacy Nights and supplying and discussing ways to encourage and build successful readers because one never knows when families are ready to receive and use the information.

Levels 6–9

Joshua made rapid progress through the next three reading levels. Students at this stage have many of the print knowledge skills in place, a set of basic sight words, some knowledge of decoding, and some idea of how to use meaning derived from the text. Books at this stage provide more lines per page, increased difficulty of words, a greater variety of words, and a more developed story line that includes a problem and solution.

I encouraged self-talk (i.e., talking oneself through a process), and I began to see evidence of Joshua's self-talk while he read orally.

"Um, I know this...," Joshua said as he thought about a strategy to employ. He tried many different strategies—including getting a running start, flipping back to another page where he had seen the word previously, and pausing to examine the picture or beginning sound again—and then he'd get the word right. Sometimes he still required a prompt to get him going in the right direction; however, overall, his hesitations were shorter as he began to employ strategies more on his own. The best part was his strong use of incorporating meaning as a strategy for confirmation.

During Joshua's reading time with these levels, I provided a variety of activities structured to help strengthen his comprehension. After reading *Blackberries* (Randell, 1996b), we returned to the text to look for important points. Joshua marked with a sticky note each page that stated an important point and discussed why that information was important to the story. Overall, he located four different important points in *Blackberries*:

1. They [Mother Bear and Papa Bear] lost their baby. (p. 9)
2. They find him in the bushes. (p. 13)
3. They ask what happened to the blueberries. (p. 15)
4. Baby Bear says the blueberries are in his tummy. (p. 16)

Although these were important points, we added pertinent instruction in areas such as using character names instead of pronouns and attending to details. With several other books, Joshua was required to formulate a prediction regarding what might happen in the story based on a picture walk through part of the book. His predictions were all plausible. Joshua then had to read the complete story to find out what actually happened. After he read the real ending, I had him compare the story ending to his prediction. We discussed how they were the same or different. All these activities required action on his part and a commitment to a verbal answer.

To help him relate characters to their actions, after reading several other books I asked him to tell me the main characters and what they did. I recorded this information as he shared it.

After many of these comprehension boosters, Joshua had many new comprehension strategies to support his success in retelling.

Joshua's May Assessment Results

By May, Joshua's assessment scores were in stanines 8 and 9 (refer to Table 2 on page 56). He correctly represented nearly all the sounds on his dictation task. For written vocabulary, he produced 60 words in 10 minutes. These words demonstrated Joshua's competence in using short vowels. Joshua also correctly used the two-letter combinations *ar*, *oy*, *sh*, *ay*, *er*, and *ou* and the three-letter combination *est*. He demonstrated that he could expand his repertoire of words by repeated use of a pattern with a change in beginning consonants. Joshua could also apply the final silent *e* to make a long vowel sound in a word. He still showed some inconsistencies and limited use of the two-letter combinations *oa*, *ea*, and *ew*. However, at the beginning of the year, he could only write four words, and during this assessment I had to stop him at the 10-minute time limit after he had written 60 words—all of which he could read back to me.

In addition, Joshua read level 9 books at instructional level and could do a retelling without prompting with 66% accuracy. With prompting, this score could climb to the upper 70s or higher. However, Joshua's organization, use of detail, and vocabulary were still his weakest areas in retelling. Therefore, our pertinent instruction would continue to focus on these areas.

Joshua was able to read *What Seahorse Saw* (Bernard, 1996), a level 1.5 book from the Watch Me Read books of our Houghton Mifflin series, with 96% accuracy. He appeared a bit hesitant at first, subvocalizing unfamiliar words, wanting to be sure before saying the words aloud. His fluency picked up as he continued with the text and became aware of the language patterns it used. He used the strategies of skipping an unknown word, reading on, and returning to it. He cross-checked, attempting to monitor his reading for meaning.

Joshua still needed to improve his fluency, continue choosing from and integrating reading strategies, and learn how to better respond to questions. However, his greatest need for development was still in the area of comprehension. Although he employed meaning while reading orally—as demonstrated by his use of the strategies of skipping an unknown word, reading on, and returning to it; monitoring for meaning; and self-correcting—this did not always carry over to understanding of the text and responses to questions about what he had read. For example, he struggled to respond to the questions I asked about *What Seahorse Saw*. He still made comments such as "I don't know," "What?" "Who?" and "I forgot," even when prompted to think about the question and answer before responding. Perhaps Joshua was still exerting most of his energy on reading the text, or perhaps he was anxious about giving the correct answer.

Although Joshua did not exit from the LEAP program during his first-grade year, I felt he had acquired many of the skills basic to moving along the reading continuum. Joshua's next steps would include more time on task reading and additional work on comprehension.

Follow-Up

Joshua returned to Sun Valley Elementary School for second grade. At the beginning of the year when I saw him in the halls, he always acknowledged my hellos but was still rather shy.

Joshua, along with all second graders who had been a part of LEAP the year before, was invited to "Morning Hop In and Read," a 15–20-minute period of time Monday through Thursday mornings before school. These students used specially issued "Hop In and Read" frog passes and came to our LEAP classroom to spend time reading either by themselves or to Mrs. Martin or me. The students who came got to choose their books to read, and we always made sure they read at least one book to one of us. They began with books at the level at which they had left off, then marveled at the fact that they had moved ahead many levels in these books and took it upon themselves to challenge themselves to continually higher levels. We did not plan for instruction, but if a student stalled out for an extended time while reading, Mrs. Martin or I might suggest a tried but true reading strategy: "Try skipping the word and reading on" or "What word would make sense?"

Unfortunately, Joshua's bus usually arrived just shortly before the start of school. However, he did show up in the LEAP classroom for a special few minutes of reading time several times throughout the year.

Just before the second grading period, Joshua sought me out in the halls. With a loud voice and beaming smile he announced, "Mrs. Wesley, Mrs. Wesley, I'm getting straight A's!"

"That's wonderful, Joshua!" I exclaimed.

Joshua's classroom teacher affirmed that although our district doesn't give letter grades, Joshua was having general success in his academics. This was a far cry from where Joshua had begun his first-grade year.

My hope is that Joshua will continue to get the extra support he needs. Although he had made progress with many of the reading strategies during his time in the LEAP program, the reading material through the grades gets more complicated and it appears he may require continued or occasional support to continue to master the reading strategies, especially in comprehension.

Conclusion

The points of action were a powerful influence on Joshua's reading growth over the course of our year together. Planning and attempting numerous opportunities for conversation led to engaged and meaningful conversations with him. Allowing Joshua to choose books to read or reread and sentences to write provided him with ownership in our lessons and follow-up practices. Critical observation of Joshua's task performance enabled me to plan pertinent instruction. It also allowed me to "meet" Joshua where he was and help move him to the next level. Conversations with his classroom teacher and meetings with his mother in which we exchanged information regarding what strategies to try and what to reinforce kept us on a common path and united us in planning for Joshua's success, thus giving him the consistent support he needed. Joshua's desire to read became evident throughout the year, especially when it related to a personal interest or success with a strategy. Consequently, a sincere purpose for his reading allowed Joshua to blossom.

Chapter 4

A Year With Brianna: A Different Kind of Success Story

Carolyn's LEAP group is quietly reading a selection when one group member, Brianna, exclaims, "We don't have to read this part because it is in a different language!"

Thinking about this comment, Carolyn looks over Brianna's shoulder and decides it is time for a lesson on italics.

Brianna is a second grader who rarely hesitates to figure out things to her own satisfaction. She has her own ideas and opinions about the way things are—or should be—and shares them freely. Brianna holds the reigns on her world tightly. This need for control and clarity probably stems from facing so many difficult times during her early years. At the age of two, she was diagnosed with and treated for leukemia. In Brianna's kindergarten year, her mother found herself unable to care for her children and legal custody was transferred to an aunt and uncle.

Changes and disruptions in her home life and school life negatively affected Brianna's ability to focus on academics. She attended a first grade in which two teachers job-shared until after Christmas. Then a third teacher was hired, and Brianna entered another new situation. Finally, Brianna came to Canyon Elementary School for second grade—where she experienced more stability and consistency. This was where her different kind of success story began.

Initial Assessments

Based on Brianna's initial LEAP testing period, her overall scores placed her second from last of all the second graders tested. Table 3 documents Brianna's initial testing results (September), which indicate a variety of weaknesses but also a number of strengths from which we could begin our work.

The Oral Reading Analysis showed that Brianna used a bit of phonetic analysis strategy, but in isolation from other strategies. She did not appear to follow the story line, to expect logical statements, or to anticipate what the author would say next. She also was not using her own oral language structure to cross-check the "sound" of what she was reading. She even totally ignored the pictures.

Table 3
Brianna's Assessment Results

Date	Dictation Task	Letter Identification	Ohio Word Test	Phoneme Awareness	Writing Vocabulary	Oral Reading Analysis
September						
Raw Score	34/37	53/54	10/20	29/35	18	Level 1
Percentage	92%	98%	50%	83%		71%
Stanine	7	7	5		4	—
December						
Raw Score	37/37		17/20		27	Level 7
Percentage	100%	—	85%	—		99%
Stanine	9	—	8	—	6	—
March						
Raw Score	36/37		20/20		46	Level 9
Percentage	97%	—	100%	—		94%
Stanine	9	—	9	—	9	—
May						
Raw Score	36/37		20/20		35	Level 13
Percentage	97%	—	100%	—		94%
Stanine	9	—	9	—	7	—

Reflection Point 4.1 _____

Based on this data, what do you think are Brianna's strengths? Remember that these are first-grade assessments and Brianna is a second grader. What does she struggle with? List any other information you would like to have before planning instruction. Based on this analysis, how would you begin your work with Brianna?

It was clear that Brianna's reading skills were well below her second-grade classmates' average, and thus she qualified for our LEAP program. Her aunt and uncle were cooperative and returned the signed permission forms and compacts within one day. The compacts signed by Brianna, her guardians, the classroom teacher, and the LEAP team provided the framework for the consistent support necessary for Brianna's growth in reading.

Exploration Sessions

We spent our first few exploration sessions completing activities intended to help us learn a bit more about each other. One of the activities involved making words using the letters of a larger word. From the letters in the word _spider_, Brianna generated the words _I_ and _rip_ independently, and _is_, _dip_, _pie_, and _Sid_ with some prompting. She also made _id_ for _I'd_ and _er_ for _ear_.

During our second activity, I read aloud _The Tiny Woman's Coat_ (Cowley, 1996c) and Brianna retold the same story in her own words. Brianna recounted only 4 out of the possible 14 important points from the story. She did not sequentially present the ones she did recall. After Brianna delivered the 4th point, she began making up dialogue for the main character, which brought the story to an abrupt and incorrect, but logical, end.

In the story, a tiny woman who lives in a forest needs a coat but has no materials to make one. Each time she bemoans not having something, a character from the story provides it, and, in the end, she is able to make a fine coat. In Brianna's retelling, the woman wanted a coat but had no buttons, thread, or needle and then went back and forth between "Where will I get them from?" and "I don't know how to make one." Brianna ended her version of the story with, "Then she said, 'I don't know. The end.'"

It is interesting that, later, when I asked Brianna to name as many characters from the story as she remembered, she named four out of a possible six. When I asked her why she hadn't mentioned all these characters during her retelling of the story, her answer was, "I don't know...I don't want to." As for being able to identify the problem and solution of the story, Brianna's response was consistent with her retelling. She easily and accurately identified the problem but did not recognize the solution. She said that the problem was never solved. It appeared that Brianna, normally a verbal child, saw no purpose for applying her verbal skills to this task. Learning to identify the solution to the problem in a story became a pertinent point of instruction during the year.

One last activity was a 16-word spelling test, Assessment of Word-Recognition Knowledge and Spelling Stages. The words each contained only one syllable but were composed of a variety of single- and multiple-letter phonograms. The results showed that Brianna was aware of letters representing sounds but was not yet able to use spelling conventions such as a final silent *e*. For example, she wrote *l-a-t* for *late*, *g-e-s-s* for *geese*, and *l-r-n-d* for *learned*. This information led me to prepare some pertinent instruction on spelling conventions.

Meeting Brianna's Needs

So, what did I discover about Brianna during this special time, and how did these observations guide my instruction? I found out that she was not motivated to improve her reading skills for the sake of improvement; she lacked purpose. If she felt like it, she would work to accommodate the wishes of the teacher. If she didn't, she simply refused to exert any effort. For this reason, my most important task was to offer a purpose that would appeal to Brianna and keep her motivated consistently.

Finding Motivation in Meaningful Conversation

When I considered her unsettled early school years, Brianna's uncon-cerned attitude did not surprise me. For this same reason, I knew that the one-to-one time built into the LEAP program was a powerful moti-vating factor. This time I shared with only Brianna provided her some of the attention she needed. She could discuss stories with me on a more personal level. We engaged in meaningful conversation. I fo-cused on and pointed out her positive achievements. She could always express her opinions and know she was heard and her opinions would be responded to.

Actually, expressing her opinions during readings was commonplace for Brianna. She would pull her chair up next to mine and begin reading. After a while, she would stop, look at me, and express an opinion about what a particular character had done or should do. This, of course, was desirable behavior because it revealed her involvement with the story. For example, while reading *Mr. Grump* (Cowley, 1996b), a book about a grouchy husband and a wise, empathetic wife, Brianna expressed her opinion that if Mrs. Grump had kissed Mr. Grump sooner, he wouldn't have been so mean to everyone else. "Why didn't she just kiss him in the first place?" she asked.

At other times, a passage would remind her of something in her own life and she would recount events unrelated to the story. Once, she was reading a story about the different things a character could see from up in a tree, and Brianna started talking about a game she had played with her cousin in her backyard. Bringing her back to a story without dis-counting her ideas or having her feel she had done something incor-rectly was always a challenge.

Reflection Point 4.2

How much reading time should be allowed for personal response and how much should be reserved for learning and practicing strategies and responding to more academic purposes? Justify your decision.

Having my full and undivided attention during the one-to-one time was definitely one of several factors that proved motivating for Brianna. I hoped that eventually, however, Brianna would read because of some internal motivation, some personal purpose. Perhaps she would want to see what would happen next, or she would really like an author's sense of humor, or she would want to learn more about a certain topic. My goal was to see her read voluntarily and to set her own personal purposes, with or without an audience. At this point, however, I was happy to provide the attention Brianna craved and participate in meaningful—or, at times, tangential—conversation with her.

Finding Motivation in Choices

Another motivating factor for Brianna was the opportunity the program offered her to make choices. She could choose which book to take home, which color of sentence strip paper she wanted to use each day, whether to write about a particular character from a story or the plot in her draft book, whether to use a pencil or marker, and which color marker she wanted to use. Making these types of choices early in the program gave Brianna a sense of ownership and control over her situation, which she clearly enjoyed.

For example, there were times when Brianna disregarded my suggestions regarding books I felt she would enjoy, choosing her own reading material to take home instead. On one occasion she wanted to read the book *Brittany the Brontosaurus* (Dee & Scott, 1993), which was above her reading level. Because of her unrelenting insistence, I allowed her to take the book home with a special bookmark in it indicating to her guardians that the book was difficult and they could help her. Brianna did manage to work her way through the book and loved it. When she returned it, she voluntarily shared her favorite pictures and passages with me.

The book describes what Brittany does each day of the week. Brianna shared her favorite parts with animation and confidence. I think the rhyme and rhythm of the verse contributed to her enjoyment.

"Brittany took her dog

for a jog." (p. 1)

and

"Brittany flew a kite

out of sight." (p. 5)

A book's illustrations, the print size or type, the topic, or the writing style can capture a student's interest. It can make the student's desire match the teacher's overall purpose for reading. Brianna's sense of pleasure demonstrated the incredible power of internal motivation stemming from this opportunity to make her own choices and set her own purpose. Researcher Donald Graves recommends that readers self-select about 80% of the texts they read. Graves notes, "We know that readers get better at reading when they choose books they can and want to read" (as cited in Harvey & Goudvis, 2000, p. 29).

*Reflection Point 4.3*_____

Create a T-chart by filling an entire sheet of paper with the letter *T*. On the left side of the paper, list the possible advantages of limiting a student to an independent reading level. On the right side, list the disadvantages. List any considerations that should be taken into account when allowing a student to choose a book to read.

Finding Motivation in Pertinent Instruction and Consistent Support

A third great motivator for Brianna was the feeling of success she experienced because of carefully planned pertinent instruction. Pertinent instruction takes the student from the known to the unknown in manageable steps. Mrs. Waffle, the RIA, and I were aware of Brianna's strengths and offered pertinent instruction that made it possible for Brianna to begin accumulating successes.

For example, in November Brianna wrote a sentence about the book *Vera's Vegetables* (Zane, 1998), which she had just finished reading, in her draft book. The story reads, "Vera made a volcano from her vegetables.

'Eat your vegetables,' said Mom" (p. 3). "Vera made a castle. 'Eat your vegetables,' said Mom" (p. 7). Among other things, we had spent time scrutinizing the word *vegetables* with Elkonin sound boxes. Before she left the LEAP classroom for the day, Brianna looked at me smugly and said, "I can spell *vegetables* by myself, v-e-g-e-t-a-b-l-e-s." "Great!" I responded, giving her a high five. A proud Brianna then returned to her class, where she asked her teacher to let her to share something she learned that day with her classmates. Granted permission, she confidently spelled the "giant" word and awed her peers. The next day she told me she had shared her new prowess with her family and that they had been quite impressed. "See," she bragged, "I can still remember it...v-e-g-e-t-a-b-l-e-s!" The lesson involved reading the word, but Brianna herself took it further and learned to spell the word. She did this independently and confidently. The pertinence of the lesson allowed Brianna to be successful, and the consistent support of her classroom teacher and her family of her efforts in LEAP added greater excitement to her success.

Each little success built on a previous one and led to Brianna wanting to try more books because she knew she could read them and because she found it satisfying to improve and succeed. Each little success made the challenge of reading more conquerable and fun for her.

Of all the things I learned about Brianna's needs during the initial testing, how to motivate her was probably the key to the rest of her learning. The one-to-one attention and opportunities for meaningful conversations gave Brianna a purpose to read. The opportunities to make choices gave her a sense of control over her learning. Pertinent instruction built a pattern of success and helped her learn to expect success and be willing to take risks. In addition, all the players on Brianna's journey to literacy offered consistent support and encouragement.

Brianna's First Group Focus Lesson

After completing the testing and exploring activities, Brianna's LEAP group and I had our first group focus lesson. Brianna's group included Rick, Clark, and Taylor. Brianna was quite aware that, aside from me, she was the only girl in the group. This situation, along with the discovery that the boys were already best of buddies, made our first group focus

lesson a bit awkward for Brianna. There was an advantage to this, however. Rick, who had participated in LEAP during the previous year, wanted to appear knowledgeable in front of Clark and Taylor. Clark and Taylor
also wanted to appear bright and successful in front of Rick. Thus, the
students themselves set a positive work tone from the start. Brianna's
behavior and participation reflected a lack of confidence, though. She
was quiet, uncommonly soft-spoken, and did not put forth a strong effort. The very thing that was motivating the three boys appeared to be
intimidating to Brianna. Over the next few days, Brianna and I had several meaningful conversations to help her cope with her feelings. These
chats along with her increasing familiarity and positive experiences with
the group helped to alleviate this problem.

Reflection Point 4.4

Generate some ideas about how to work with children so they
develop positive, respectful attitudes toward one another.
Develop some activities that encourage cooperative and collab-
orative behaviors and also ensure the safety and inclusion of each
child in the group.

This first lesson included the rhyme "Bonjour, Mr. McGrue" from
Sherman's Book of Nursery Rhymes (Rap & Young, 1991, pp. 25–27). It
is a lively verse calling for lots of expression, and the children spontaneously joined in on anticipated rhymes.

My objective was for the students to visualize what was happening
in the text as we read and then to share their imaginings. I would read
up to a particular stanza, and we would talk about how we visualized it
on our own "mental TVs." In one verse, we pictured Sherman dancing,
slipping, and landing in France. We talked about how Sherman may
have felt finding himself in a foreign country so suddenly. I asked the students to show how Sherman must have felt using only facial expres-
sions. Brianna enthusiastically participated with the boys, making
wonderful facial contortions followed by much laughter.

In the beginning, however, the students' verbal descriptions were somewhat sparse and incomplete. Fortunately, listening to each other provided a kind of peer modeling that fed their imaginations. By the time we reached the end of the rhyme, the students' conversation included not only the food they imagined at the final picnic but also the smells, sounds, and details of the surroundings. The silliness of the rhyme, the opportunity for physical participation, and the meaningful sharing of ideas made this a great first activity for everyone in the group.

As the second graders prepared to return to their classroom, each child chose one or two books at his or her independent reading level to take home and read to a designated listener. Brianna's book was a level 1. Clark and Taylor chose level 7 books, and Rick chose a level 13 book.

Brianna was acutely aware from the start that her books were at a different level than the others in her group, and that discouraged her. I explained that all students in LEAP were different, that different students read at different levels, and that they would change levels at different times. These conversations helped a bit, but it was when Brianna saw herself improving that she realized she was in control of her own learning. This awareness gave her a new purpose for reading, and she was a much happier student.

Reflection Point 4.5

List some things a teacher can do and/or have students do to draw students' attention away from the level of the books they are reading and focus them instead on their developing strengths and increased abilities to choose and use strategies. Share your ideas with a colleague.

Overall, this first focus lesson showed that, in spite of their differences, Brianna, Rick, Clark, and Taylor learned with and from one another. The small-group format allowed and encouraged the students to participate in more meaningful conversation than would be possible or desirable in a classroom. As Brianna became familiar with the group members and experienced successes, she became an enthusiastic and active member of the group. Despite the underlying current of competition among the boys, an atmosphere of acceptance prevailed. I worked to encourage and maintain this atmosphere throughout the year.

Group Work With Mrs. Waffle

Brianna, Clark, and Rick spent the next day working with Mrs. Waffle while Taylor worked one-to-one with me. Mrs. Waffle's small-group session began with each student silently reading a book of his or her choice. The students spent the following five minutes writing in their draft books, an activity Brianna enjoyed most of the time. Unfortunately, after a minute or so of writing, Brianna reverted to chatting. This off-task behavior caused her to need more work time than was allotted for the activity. So, when time was up, she became disgruntled because she was not finished. In this case, experience was the best teacher, and after analysis of the situation with Mrs. Waffle, Brianna learned to stay on task—most of the time.

Next, the group focused on word work. This first day, Mrs. Waffle introduced the students to the word wall by playing a game that incorporated the words on the wall called "I'm thinking of a word...." Word wall games became favorite activities for Brianna and the rest of the group because they were more like playing than working. The word wall also came in handy during writing time to help students help themselves with spelling.

The small-group session ended with a 15-minute review of a story from the second-grade class work. The students had already read the story in their classroom and spent this time discussing aspects of the story. This activity helped the students feel more confident and participate more willingly in the classroom. This activity also enhanced students' story comprehension by building on previous learning.

Mrs. Waffle incorporated all the points of action into her sessions. The students chose their own books, chose their own sentence topics, and often chose between several appropriate activities. All the lessons were pertinent to the needs of the students as determined and planned by Mrs. Waffle, the classroom teacher, and me. In this way, the purposes of Mrs. Waffle's lessons were the same as those of the classroom teacher and mine. Her support of the students' reading development was consistent with my work and that of the classroom teacher. Mrs. Waffle often prepared lessons to reinforce the students' reading work in the classroom. The students engaged in many meaningful conversations as they worked on the various lessons together, and every activity served the purpose of increasing each student's reading ability. The use of the five points of action made Mrs. Waffle's work with Brianna and the rest of the students positive and productive.

Our First One-to-One Session

Based on her initial testing results, my first goals for Brianna were to help her develop a larger sight-word vocabulary and then to use this vocabulary by transferring letter–sound matches to new words and identifying word families, or "chunks," within words.

I made our first one-to-one session pertinent to Brianna's needs by focusing on developing her sight-word vocabulary. We began with a set of 10 common word flashcards (Easy Sight Words by Frank Schaffer Publications). The words include *after*, *again*, *airplane*, *any*, *apple*, *baby*, *ball*, *bed*, *best*, and *could*. When Brianna did not recognize or decode a word on a card, we looked on the back of the flashcard where the same word was used in a sentence. Brianna used the context clues in the sentence to clarify the meaning of the unknown word. Then, she thought of words that carried the correct meaning and cross-checked her guesses using letter–sound matching.

For example, the word *could* was difficult for Brianna to decode in isolation. She turned to the back of the card that read, "I could run fast." Brianna read, "I blank run fast." We talked about what the writer was trying to say and which word would make sense and begin with /c/. Brianna said that *can* started with /c/ and would make sense. Then, she examined the letters used in the word to see if they matched the other sounds in the word she was saying. Brianna noticed that *can* could not be right because the word on the card ended with /d/. Next, we brainstormed other words that would make sense, sound right, and look right. Brianna was able to come up with the correct word, *could*. Her ability to read this word was based heavily on her knowledge of what made sense and what sounded correct and then cross-checking using letter–sound matching.

Because she had difficulty with the word *airplane*, we also discussed compound words. Then, we ended our word study with the *-est* family, taken from the sight word *best* in the word list. Brianna was quite pleased to be able to generate eight words from the *-est* family on her own. As she thought of words, she kept track of them by writing the words on a white board. Brianna was always pleased to write on the white board with markers. She carefully copied words in her best printing, listed words from the same word family, and made sound boxes with perfectly straight lines to analyze words she had difficulty with. She happily explained what she was doing and used a marker as a pointer. I think she felt like she was the teacher!

Along with strategies for identifying unknown words, we worked on developing a more extensive sight vocabulary during this part of the lesson. Once she decoded each word, Brianna practiced reading these cards until she was able to "fast flash." This meant that she read all the words on the cards with little or no hesitation.

In this session, we spent more than the three minutes of allotted time on word study. I occasionally spent extended time on something that seemed more pertinent to the child's learning at a particular point. Brianna needed a lot of work on decoding skills and sight vocabulary, so we spent more time on word study in the beginning.

We touched on a significant number of strategies during this lesson. Although she was not adept at using them yet, Brianna and I built shared reference points for strategies that could be discussed in future interactions as needed. Our conversation could address Brianna's immediate need, be personal, and allow time for exploration as well as application. We could see some of the results of combining pertinent instruction with meaningful conversation: Brianna recognized more words by sight, increasing her fluency; was willing to risk trying higher-level books; began using more strategies to solve word problems; and was able to better comprehend stories.

Following the word-study activity, Brianna completed an Oral Reading Analysis. Using the level 2 book *Run* (Cutting, 1996), which she had checked out and read the previous Monday, I scripted an oral reading analysis of her reading. Brianna scored 98%, indicating an independent reading level. Her reading did, however, lack expression and fluency. When she came to a word she did not recognize, she made some efforts at sounding out the word, looked at the pictures, and guessed. She never figured out the word *leopard*, and she read *animals* instead of *rhinoceros*. I attributed her high score to the predictability of the text, rather than to her actual reading ability. So even though her oral reading analysis score indicated that Brianna read the book at a high instructional level, I knew she was not reading independently at this level.

Composing a sentence after our oral reading experience proved a difficult undertaking for Brianna. Because she did not seem to know where to begin, we ended up discussing the concept of a sentence and orally composing sentences that I wrote on the white board. Because of time restraints, Brianna did not write in her draft book. I found it frustrating not to be able to complete all the components of the lesson, but at the same time, I did not want to stop work on one component when I felt the goal of that part of the lesson hadn't been completed.

The new book I chose for her was a level 3 book, *Teeny Tiny Tina* (Butler, 1989). This book has helpful pictures and predictable text. It presents good opportunities for learning strategy use. Brianna needed repeated help with the name Teeny Tiny Tina, had difficulty decoding some of the words because she did not yet possess strong letter–sound matching skills, and did not use the picture clues to their full advantage. I pointed out picture cues and modeled how I would use the rimes in words to help decode them. Brianna, however, was not interested in the story line and wanted to move on as soon as she perceived that we had finished.

"I want that book," she said upon completing *Teeny Tiny Tina*. She was pointing to the Big Book *Charlie the Dinosaur* (Child, 1992), with a picture of a T-Rex dressed in a colorful baseball cap and a tie. When I saw her desire to read the book, even though it was about 10 levels beyond her current independent level, we brought it to the table and worked through the story together. With support, Brianna read the book of her choice with strong purpose, never losing focus.

When we finished, Brianna immediately went to the book boxes and picked another book above her level, *Brittany the Brontosaurus*. As mentioned earlier, I allowed her to take this book home. We did compromise, however. Brianna agreed to take *Teeny Tiny Tina* home to read to her family, unaided. I agreed to let her take *Brittany the Brontosaurus* home and have her family help her with the difficult areas. I also sent a note of explanation to her guardians so they would not be confused about the increased level of difficulty of this new book. Everyone was happy. The following week, Brianna read *Teeny Tiny Tina* for her oral reading analysis with 97% accuracy and improved fluency.

Overall, during our first one-to-one session we varied from the actual planned schedule, but the adjustments were pertinent to Brianna's needs and helped increase her motivation. They also gave us opportunities to begin our work on letter–sound matching, sight words, and reading strategies.

Assessment Results

In December, Mrs. Waffle and I administered assessments to evaluate students' progress, strengths, and needs. Because our pertinent instruction had focused on developing a stronger sight-word vocabulary, we were happy to see that Brianna had progressed from stanine 5 to 8 on the Ohio Word Test, from stanine 4 to 6 on the Writing Words Test, and from stanine 7 to 9 on the Dictation Test (refer to Table 3 on page 94). Brianna also moved from an instructional below level Reading Recovery book level 1 to a level 7. We were pleased to see progress she had made, but because all these tests use first-grade norms, we still had a lot of work to accomplish.

September to December Word Work: Finding Motivation in Games

As I reviewed the results of the tests, I reflected on some of the activities Brianna completed. The phonics program used in our district is based on 70 phoneme-letter units called phonograms. These are minimal speech units, not blends. They include the letters of the alphabet plus some multiple-letter units such as *ea* and *ng*. Most of Brianna's word-study lessons from September through December were based on work with multiple-letter vowel phonograms because they seemed to be a major stumbling block in her decoding attempts.

In planning pertinent instruction, I chose phonograms for a particular day's work from errors recorded during analysis of Brianna's oral reading and from errors made during her practice with flashcards. Repeated practice was necessary for Brianna to be able to fluently read words containing certain phonograms.

We used teacher-made board games to make this practice pertinent and fun (see Figures 11, 12, and 13). Brianna loved to play the games. "You know I'm going to beat you again if we get to play a game, Mrs. Bryan!" she beamed. As often as I could without getting caught, I organized the cards to provide the practice I wanted for Brianna and to ensure that she would win. She only caught me one time. "No cheating, Mrs. Bryan!" was her comment as she wagged a finger at me.

The games were on file folders and laminated so that the information on the blank squares that formed the path of the game was erasable. I filled in the blank squares with whichever phonograms, word parts, or words I wanted to work on that day, then erased the squares and filled them in with different phonograms, word parts, or words on another day. Some of the squares contained special instructions such as "Move ahead 2," "Go back 2," "Get 1 free turn," or "Lose 1 turn." These instructions added a little more excitement to the games.

Most games worked with only two or three phonograms or rimes so that the game would not take too much time to complete, would provide pointed practice on specific phonograms or rimes, and would provide clear reference points for Brianna. (Box 4.1 presents resources for additional games involving word study.) "Look! There are the letters we had in our game!" exclaimed a surprised Brianna as she read from her book. After that first recognition, Brianna made it a point whenever she read to look for words containing the phonograms we had used during our games. She was delighted when she found familiar phonograms. We related the experience to finding a buried treasure. A few other times, Brianna even approached me on the playground with words she read in her classroom containing our game phonograms. Each of these discoveries was another small step on her path to literacy.

Figure 11
Sound Match Practice Game

Sound Match focuses on the different sounds a particular phonogram could represent. For example, to practice the sounds of the phonogram *ou*—which can stand for any one of four different sounds in (1) *round*, (2) *four*, (3) *you*, or (4) *country*—mark the squares on the game path with four words that exemplify each of the four sounds. Prepare game cards by writing the words on them. The game works as follows: If a player draws a card with the word *found*, the player should move his or her marker to the next square with a word containing the same sound, such as *pound*. If a player draws a card with the word *pour*, he or she moves to the next square with a word containing the same sound, such as *four*. Players continue taking turns identifying sounds around the board until one player crosses the finish line.

Figure 12
Missing Pieces Game

To practice two or three different phonograms or chunks, write them in alternating squares on the game path. Write words missing one of the phonograms or chunks on game cards. For example, to practice the rimes *at*, *ack*, and *am*, write them in the squares on the gameboard. Then, play with cards that provide initial sounds but need the rime, such as c___, l___, or d___. If more than one rime would make a real word, the player chooses the word that allows him or her to move the greatest distance. The game ends when one player crosses the finish line.

Figure 13
Vowel Match Practice Game

To practice vowel sounds, the squares on the game path should each contain a vowel—*a*, *e*, *i*, *o*, or *u*. Players then take turns drawing a card containing a word missing a vowel phonogram. Each player needs to figure out the possible words it could be and then moves to the square containing the missing vowel phonogram. For example, if a player draws a card showing f_n, the player identifies the word as *fan*, *fin*, or *fun* and then moves to the square with *a*, *i*, or *u*, whichever allows the player to move the greatest distance. The game continues until a player crosses the finish line.

Box 4.1
Resources for Word Study Games

Bear, D.R., Invernizzi, M., Templeton, S., & Johnston, F. (2004). *Words their way: Word study for phonics, vocabulary, and spelling instruction* (3rd ed.). Upper Saddle River, NJ: Pearson.

Blevins, W. (1999). *Quick-and-easy learning games: Phonics*. New York: Scholastic.

Johns, J.L., & Lenski, S.D. (1997). *Improving reading: A handbook of strategies* (2nd ed.). Dubuque, IA: Kendall/Hunt.

Julio, S. (2001). *15 fun and easy games for young learners: Reading. Reproducible, easy-to-play learning games that help kids build essential reading skills*. New York: Scholastic.

Morrow, L.M. (2002). *The literacy center: Contexts for reading and writing* (2nd ed.). Portland, ME: Stenhouse.

Ramsey, M.K. (2000). *Phonics games kids can't resist: 25 lively learning games that make teaching phonics easy and fun*. New York: Scholastic.

September to December Reading: Relying on Meaning

From the beginning, Brianna tried to make sense of what she was reading. Her first attempt usually reflected the correct meaning of the word, but when she found she was not correct, she became flustered and reverted to the ineffective word sounding strategies on which she had depended at the beginning of the year.

Brianna often looked for meaning but was not graphophonically or syntactically correct. Her incorrect responses sometimes made sense, but they did not match the phonograms in the text or follow a correct language pattern. For example, while trying to read the word *ledge* in *The Long, Long Tail* (Cowley, 1996a), Brianna responded with the word *sill*, which is correct in meaning but does not match the phonograms in the book. Brianna became frustrated when she knew she was not correct. She reread the word as *led*, which more closely matched the graphophonic clues but made no sense. In *Kitty and the Birds* (Randell, 1996e), her only error was *chirp* for *cheep*—six times. Her sense of correct meaning was present, but she missed the graphophonic cues. Reading *the* for *a* was another common graphophonic error she made.

Brianna was not cross-checking for letter–sound matching. This did not cause a comprehension problem in the predictable texts we were using at the time; however, to be a successful reader, Brianna needed to read for meaning and cross-check for letter–sound matching. Other errors Brianna made included *sit* for *sat*, *makes* for *made*, and *eats* for *ate*. Each of these errors demonstrated Brianna's comprehension of the text but also her inaccurate grasp of language structure. She needed to be able to combine multiple strategies in order to advance to higher-level reading tasks.

During these first four months, Mrs. Waffle and I spent time encouraging Brianna to continue to not only expect logical meaning in her reading but also to make use of graphophonic and structural cues to cross-check as she read. By December she was still relying mainly on meaning, had added a consistent use of picture cues, and was better at letter–sound matching, but was not yet fluent.

In mid-November, when we prepared to move from level 4 to level 5 books, Brianna revealed some lingering insecurity by responding, "That book is too hard. I can't read it." After a little coaxing though, Brianna read *Good for You* (Cowley, 1994) with only two errors: *fresh* and *fruit*.

Reflection Point 4.6

Examine some children's books. Which factors about them could cause a reader to either embrace that book confidently or push it away as too great a risk? Also, explore which characteristic(s) about a particular child affects that child's response to a particular book.

Despite the fact that Brianna was only in second grade, she was already stuck in her method of solving reading problems. She continued to rely on meaning largely to the exclusion of graphophonic and syntactic clues, even though her teachers presented and modeled the flexible use of multiple strategies. Brianna's resistance to changing her problem-solving strategies reflected her fear of taking risks.

We planned to continue to help Brianna experience the successes she needed to increase her willingness to expand her strategy use.

Reflection Point 4.7

As you listen to a beginning reader, can you determine what type of strategies the child is using and which she is not using? Tape-record a child reading. List some indicators that show what clues the child is using. Is the child leaning more heavily toward grapho-phonic clues, syntactic clues, or semantic clues? How can you tell if the child is not using certain types of clues? How can you use this information to guide pertinent instruction?

September to December Writing: Learning to Take Risks

One of our more entertaining lessons was with the sentence Brianna wrote as a summary of the controlled vocabulary book *Fuzz and the Buzz* (Cushman, 1990). She had been having trouble decoding words with the short sound of the vowel *u*. Therefore, I chose this book to give her extra practice with *u* sounds. Her summary sentence read, *Fuzz hugs and hums and tugs and runs*. We enjoyed the rhythm of the sentence, and after I rewrote it on a sentence strip and cut apart the words, we tried different ways of ordering the verbs to see which sounded best. Brianna enjoyed manipulating the words in this game-like format. This activity was motivational and an effective method for helping Brianna strengthen her language and writing skills.

During our sentence writing time, Brianna sometimes worked on letter–sound matching with sound boxes when she didn't know how to spell a word. At other times, I gave her the magnetic letters for a word she was having difficulty with and she ordered them as she sounded out the word. During this time, we also talked about and practiced using correct capitalization, end punctuation, serial commas, and quotation marks.

Mrs. Waffle and I spent the first nine weeks of the school year expanding Brianna's sight vocabulary, providing her with a variety of new reading strategies, and improving or replacing some ineffectual reading strategies. We also focused on making reading and writing fun as well as purposeful. All our conversations helped Brianna internalize new ways to view and take control of her own reading. Finally, because our instruction was pertinent, the games were fun, and Brianna was involved in choosing her own goals, she had begun to experience success. Although Brianna was progressing slowly, I felt that important background was being set in place for her during this time.

As mentioned earlier, Brianna's first attempts at sentence composition were not always successful. Yet, in December, she easily composed a sentence with two prepositional phrases. She wrote, *I like my dog because my dog is nice to cats like I taught her to be.* This sentence shows an increase in Brianna's willingness to take risks. The daily draft book writing activities with Mrs. Waffle, which involved no corrections, certainly added to this willingness to take risks. A richer background in book language from increased daily reading and direct instruction concerning pertinent aspects of writing contributed to Brianna's improvement and newfound confidence.

Confidence leads a child to a greater willingness to take risks. This is a desirable transition for students to make. According to Dombey (1999), the willingness to take risks is crucial for a student learning to read: "Children need to learn confidence; a firm belief that they will learn to read. Children need to see learning to read as something normal and themselves as capable of achieving it. Teachers must have faith in their pupils' capacities" (p. 2).

She goes on to state:

> Children need to learn toleration of uncertainty. Even in the early stages a reader must be prepared to put up with not knowing exactly what is going on, what a word means, or why a character is acting in a particular way, and be prepared to find the answer by reading on. Again this attitude cannot be clearly separated from others: you are more likely to tolerate uncertainty if you are confident and convinced of the ultimate reward. (pp. 2–3)

Using the points of action helps lead students to greater confidence, to a greater willingness to take risks. Knowing the purpose of lessons and engaging in pertinent instruction helped improve Brianna's reading ability and her confidence. Brianna also was able to make choices—take risks—because of the consistent support from and meaningful conversations with teachers, family members, and peers about reading. We hoped that as Brianna became more confident, she would take more risks.

January to March Word Work: Focus on Word Parts

Mrs. Waffle and I leapt into the new year with some new and some tried-and-true word work activities. The games were still quite appealing to Brianna. They were fun, predictable, and user-friendly. Brianna enjoyed the competition with me and was confident in her abilities to succeed in the tasks required by the games. Her first question on most days was "Do we get to play a game today? Please!"

Some of our games still focused on words containing multiple-letter vowel phonograms such as *ou*, *ow*, *ew*, *ui*, *oy*, *oi*, *aw*, *au*, *oa*, and *oo* because these were hindering Brianna's fluent decoding of words. Brianna began noticing these phonograms in stories she was reading and even used her knowledge of them to decode unknown words.

About one third of the way through this quarter, I started working with Brianna on root words and word endings and on noticing how some root words had their spellings changed with the addition of an ending. Whenever a word with one or more endings attached stumped Brianna, we worked it out using sound boxes and magnetic letters. We always looked at the whole word and then the root word plus the ending, paying attention to any changes in the spelling of the root word.

After we spotlighted words with endings for several word work lessons, I introduced some new games to give Brianna practice at decoding words with endings. "Oh boy! A new game," she remarked excitedly. One game reused the same game boards we had used previously. Now, however, the squares along the game path contained word endings (see Figure 14).

Another activity involved a commercially made board game, The Crocodile's Mile by Creative Publications. The squares along the game path contain words with a variety of word endings. There are two different words on the board for each ending. I added a twist to the game to keep it challenging: When a player landed on a word, besides read-

---

Figure 14
Word Ending Games

Write three endings randomly in the blank squares of the game path. Each player receives three cards of each word ending, totaling nine cards. For example, one player's cards can include run-n*ing*, danc*ing*, hopp*ing*, jump*ed*, hop*ed*, cook*ed*, hot*ter*, fast*er*, and tall*er*. The first player rolls the dice and moves one space for an odd number or two spaces for an even number. The player then chooses a card from his or her set that has the same word ending as the space he or she is on. After reading aloud the card, the player places it on the table upside down. Each player has to have all nine cards upside down to cross the finish line. Players can move forward or backward in order to get all nine cards turned over. The game continues until a player crosses the finish line.

---

ing the word, he or she had to find the other word that rhymed with it on the board. Brianna had a difficult time at first, but she refreshed her rhyming skills about halfway through the game.

Along with multiple-letter vowel phonograms and word endings, Brianna and I also continued practicing sight words with flashcards. Instead of just drilling her with the flashcards, Brianna and I also made words using some of the sight words. One of the sight words Brianna worked with was *before*. Using the magnetic letters, she formed the words *or*, *ref*, *rob*, *of*, *for*, *bore*, *fore*, *robe*, *beef*, and *reef*. Then, she was able to figure out the "big" word that used all the letters: *before*. When we started this activity, Brianna needed some prompting for almost every word, but she became increasingly independent with continued practice.

Brianna eventually set her own personal goal for this activity. She decided to figure out the word that used all the letters before she did the shorter words. "Wait, Mrs. Bryan!" she would say when I asked her if she could make any two-letter words with the letters. "I need to get the big word first." After several lessons, Brianna succeeded when she correctly combined the letters to the word *dinosaur*. "See, I knew I could get the big word first!" she exclaimed.

Our winter word work, then, included multiple-letter vowel phonograms, word endings, roots, and sight vocabulary. This work enabled Brianna to become more aware of word structure because we clearly stated the purpose of the activities, the content of the lessons was pertinent, and the concepts were reinforced consistently by all of Brianna's classroom teachers. The activities gave her more automaticity at self-checking using letter–sound matching. She also gained more fluency in her reading because there were fewer long pauses caused by her not knowing what to do. She was successfully using more strategies in ways that were more efficient.

Learning to decode more efficiently was just one of the strategies we continued working to improve. As she read, I also encouraged her to look for the author's message, to try to anticipate what would come next in a story, and to make sense of the content. Brianna's purpose was to know and choose from a number of strategies the ones that would be most appropriate for a given reading situation.

January to March Reading: Lack of Progress

In January it was evident that Brianna still relied heavily on picture cues, relied a little more on meaning than before, and was not yet attentive to cross-checking using letter–sound matching. I also noticed that at this time Brianna began trying to read too quickly. Some examples of typical errors she made were *that* for *what*, *my* for *the*, *look* for *listened*, and *dinosaur* for *monster*.

I noticed that Brianna's reading was structurally correct more often in January, whereas the previous quarter a greater percentage of her errors had been structural. At this point, Brianna had read more than 85 LEAP books. Book language was becoming increasingly familiar to her, and thus incorrect syntax began to be more noticeable to her.

Our reading lessons focused a lot on checking for letter–sound matches. We talked about cross-checking and slowing down just enough to do so. We also did more rereading to work on fluency and expression.

By mid-February, Brianna was reading at level 8. Her speed and fluency, however, were erratic. One day she would read smoothly, the next day she would read slow and choppily, and another day she would read too quickly. She also was easily distracted and complained of many ailments during this time. Once she lamented having a bump on her foot, scratches on her knee, cold sores in her mouth, and itchy eyes—all during the same session.

Brianna wanted to take level 1 books home again. I allowed her to take these books home as long as she also took books at her independent reading level. She was satisfied with this arrangement and reread quite a few level 1, 2, and 3 books.

Reflection Point 4.8

Brianna is not alone in this desire to reread easy books. Why would students want to reread those early level books? What possible rewards could there be to a child rereading books or reading books at much lower levels than he or she is capable of reading? Consider whether allowing rereading or the reading of books that are too easy could be detrimental to a child's reading progress.

At times, however, Brianna read with great expression but, because she ignored the punctuation marks, did not change her expression from the voice of the character to the voice of the narrator. For example, while reading *Mean Soup* (Everitt, 1992), Brianna read the lines "His mother said, 'Did you thank Miss Pearl?' And Horace fell on the floor" (p. 11) as "'His mother said did you thank Miss Pearl and Horace fell on the floor?'" She did not change her expression or pause appropriately. This, of course, posed a challenge to comprehending the meaning of the lines. Following pertinent instruction in reading material with quotation marks and commas, Brianna's oral reading and comprehension improved.

Brianna's lack of progress during the third quarter was disappointing. Although she had added more strategies to her repertoire and learned to read punctuation more accurately, her fluency and rate seemed unaffected. It is hard to determine the cause for this lack of progress except for the fact that Brianna was having a more difficult time focusing and was not as motivated during this quarter. I planned to continue working with Brianna using the five points of action to help her overcome the obstacles to her reading progress.

January to March Writing:
From Basic to More Complex

During this quarter, Brianna's composition skills improved but her capitalization, punctuation, and spelling errors took up a lot of our time. In early February, Brianna wrote, *I like BuBBles. Theres Big BuBBles. Theres litel BuBBLes.* I used this opportunity to work on capitalization, punctuation, and spelling. We also talked about combining her sentences. Her three original sentences closely matched the level of text she was reading each day; however, combining the ideas of the three sentences into one sentence exposed Brianna to a more complex sentence structure and helped lay the groundwork for her reading of books with more complex sentence structures. Brianna's final sentence that day was *I like big and little bubbles.*

Several times Brianna wrote run-on sentences and our lessons then focused on naming connecting words and seeing which one sounded best. For example, she wrote the following:

First try: I like to play with baby girls they are nice.

Corrected: I like to play with baby girls because they are nice.

First try: Emma and sally and rebeca work it out now they are friends.

Corrected: Emma, Sally, and Rebecca worked it out and now they are friends.

Another lesson we worked on involved the use of unidentified pronouns. We talked about using nouns that helped the reader picture the sentence. For example, Brianna wrote the following:

First try: The Mouthe Duck cept kare of them.

Corrected: The mother duck took care of the baby ducklings.

Brianna seemed to show more improvement in her writing skills this quarter than in her reading skills. We discussed her writing quite a bit, and those meaningful conversations helped her better understand writing conventions. Lessons with Brianna were based on her writing needs as recognized by her classroom teacher, Mrs. Waffle, and me, from basic spelling patterns and punctuation to combining sentences into more complex statements. The lessons were pertinent to Brianna's needs, and she understood the purpose for each of them. Though the content of some of her sentences was specified ahead of time to help her learn how to write comments about books she had read, Brianna enjoyed writing most often when she was allowed to choose her own topic. Brianna's writing was becoming more accurate and complex in structure, which I hoped would lead to better reading comprehension in the near future.

Assessment Results: Hitting a Plateau

As her March assessment results show, Brianna progressed from stanine 8 to 9 on the Ohio Word Test and from stanine 6 to 9 on the Writing Words Test (refer to Table 3 on page 94) over the past nine weeks. She remained at stanine 9 on the Dictation Test. Although we were pleased with these improvements, we were somewhat disappointed that Brianna's actual independent reading level had only moved from level 7 to level 9. It seemed that she had reached a plateau. I discussed my concerns with Brianna's classroom teacher and Mrs. Waffle. Together we planned to encourage Brianna to read more and to verbalize her strategy use. We also decided to revisit the level of books she was choosing for home reading to be sure it was appropriate.

March to May Word Work: Focusing on Larger Word Chunks

During our last word-work sessions, we continued to focus on word endings and root words. Whenever Brianna came to a longer word she didn't recognize, we determined whether the word was a compound word or had an ending. If she identified an ending, we examined the word without the ending to see if there had been a spelling change. Once she decoded the root, Brianna added the ending back to the word.

The greatest problem Brianna had was with the ending *-ed*. This was because the ending could add a syllable or not, and it could sound like /ed/, /d/, or /t/. Because of these variables, sometimes Brianna pronounced *talked* as *talk-ted* or *laughed* as *laugh-ed*.

When she used these words in her normal speech, she had no problem with correct pronunciation. Her difficulty in reading words with this ending seemed to indicate either a lack of understanding of print or an overreliance on the use of visual clues and not enough attention to semantic clues. I felt the latter to be the case, and we worked on that imbalance during the new reading part of our sessions.

Reflection Point 4.9

Think of other types of errors that could lead you to recognize a student's unbalanced use of visual, semantic, or syntactic cues. Discuss ideas to stimulate a more balanced approach. These activities could involve choice of materials, activities, and/or prompts.

During these last months, we also were able to finish work on 100 words from the Easy Sight Words flashcards. In addition to the first 10 words listed earlier, we covered the following words:

birthday	day	from	know	open
book	dinosaur	gave	let	our
both	end	give	live	over
but	every	grass	love	paste
by	eyes	hand	made	pencil
call	far	his	many	please
came	farther	hot	may	pretty
can't	find	how	morning	ran
cold	first	if	mother	read
could	flag	just	night	right

cut	found	keep	once	round
say	sun	then	walk	who
school	take	there	want	why
sleep	talk	they	went	wish
some	tell	think	were	work
soon	thank	tree	when	would
street	that	under	where	yes
story	them	very	which	zoo

These words provided a good variety of letter combinations to use with making-words activities, categorizing activities, and word-family activities.

During making-words activities, I sometimes gave Brianna the letters of one of our words and asked her to create at least 10 words in addition to the original word. For example, when I gave her the letters *t, h, i, n, k*, she made the words *I, in, it, tin, kin, hit, kit, ink*, and *hint*. At times, Brianna combined letters into words not actually knowing they were words. For example, she did not know *kin* was a word when she put the letters together. Also, when she was given the letters for the word *round*, she did not know *urn* was a real word. Therefore, this activity provided unexpected vocabulary development, too.

During these final months of the school year, we focused more on identifying and using larger word chunks. When we worked on categorizing words, we usually grouped the words based on the number of syllables in each word. The use of word-family activities helped Brianna recognize the rimes in words and larger word chunks. For example, working with the rime *all* in *ball* helped her with other words containing the chunks *al* and *all*, such as *always, almost*, and *total*. I continued to vary our activities to keep Brianna's interest. We played games, manipulated magnetic letters, and used flashcards and sound boxes. I also spent less of the lesson time on word work and more time on our reading work.

March to May Reading: Making Progress

This period proved to be a time of more rapid progress for Brianna. She moved from level 9 in early March to level 12 by early May. She read with consistent accuracy as we moved through the levels. There also was noticeable improvement in her use of expression.

Although she had made progress, Brianna was still reading at a first-grade level. She continued to lack fluency. She would read slowly, then quickly, then slowly again. She would stop and go. Often when she stopped, she began talking about something else such as where she was going that weekend or whom she was not speaking to that day. She was still not remaining focused.

The types of errors Brianna made indicated to me that, even after many discussions regarding the use of strategies and much modeling, she was still not cross-checking. She used one strategy at a time but did not combine strategies. For example, reading *strong* for *strange* and *par* for *poor* showed Brianna's use of beginning and ending sounds but not meaning. Then, errors such as *the* for *a*, *a* for *the*, and *ruff* for *wuff* showed her the use of meaning cues or word structure but not letter–sound matching.

In an effort to demonstrate and encourage the use of multiple strategies, I planned pertinent instruction to focus on these areas. I talked to her about and had her practice thinking about what the author said. Then, we tried anticipating what the author might say next. We worked on reading past the unknown word, looking for clues, and then rereading the sentence.

During the reread of the sentence, we practiced "sliding through" the unknown word and pronouncing the sounds she did know. Then, we tried to figure out which word made sense and sounded like our pronunciation. Brianna used these strategies when she was reminded of them, yet did not use them on her own. Instead, she kept jumping from one strategy to another, and one was not enough to help her. I attempted to remedy this problem by repeatedly asking Brianna to verbalize the strategies she was using and evaluate which strategies helped her and which did not.

March to May Writing: Brianna's Writing Skills Blossom

Brianna made no capitalization or end punctuation errors during this time. She did, however, continue to need help with spelling and run-on sentences. For example, she wrote the following:

First try: The best part was wen the mom sied you are a scardy bear and it was the cids.

Corrected: The best part was when the mom said that the father was a scaredy bear, and they saw it was just the kids.

First try: Tiger is a scardy cat he is scard of a trucks and he is scard of vacuum cleaners too and mice!

Corrected: Tiger is a scaredy cat who is scared of trucks, vacuum cleaners, and mice.

We encouraged Brianna to look back in the book for spellings. In addition to simply sounding out the words, she could also try sound boxes. When necessary, I helped her with unusual spellings. Brianna's reading of a variety of books also offered her more encounters with words to support correct spellings.

From March to May, Brianna continued to improve her knowledge of different strategies, her writing skills blossomed, and her reading level improved at a faster rate than it had during the previous nine-week period. Unfortunately, although she knew various strategies, Brianna was still not adept at choosing and using appropriate ones in combination. She also was not able to read at grade level.

Focus Lessons

Throughout the year, I met with Brianna's entire group for focus lessons eight more times. I planned each lesson to provide pertinent instruction. The focus lessons provided memories or reference points for future conversations during one-to-one sessions.

During the second focus lesson, I planned to introduce the use of multiple strategies when working through unknown words, an area of confusion for all the group members. I began by reading aloud *In 1492* (Marzollo, 1991) with emphasis on the rhyming words.

Following this reading, I divided among the four students small cards on which I had written the second words of each pair of rhyming words from the verses. During the second reading, I omitted the second rhyming word from each verse. The students used memory, meaning, and rhyme to figure out the missing words. Then, they checked the words on their cards to see if any made sense and rhymed with another word in the verse. A student then held up a card and explained how he or she knew it was the correct word.

Clark had no problem with the rhyming words or the word identification. Rick also accomplished the tasks with little difficulty. Brianna and Taylor had no problem recognizing words once they were identified, but they did have trouble with rhyming and figuring out missing words.

I designed the third focus lesson to increase awareness of word endings. Often during our one-to-one sessions, I noticed Brianna and the other students omitting these endings. Therefore, I decided to provide pertinent instruction by conducting a lesson that would require students to scan words from the beginning to the end, especially noting the endings. I gave each child four cards with the same root word but with different endings. For example, one set included *jump, jumped, jumping*, and *jumper*. The first student began by identifying what was the same in each word, *jump*. Next, I dictated one of the words and the student had to use the ending to identify the card with the correct word.

Although the task seemed simple to me, it took a while for Brianna, Clark, Rick, and Taylor to identify all the letters that were the same. They named only the first two letters, then the first three letters. It actually took several rounds before all the students could identify all the letters that were the same on a given set of cards. By the end of the activity, all the students were able to identify the dictated word with the correct ending.

The next focus lesson centered on the comprehension elements of problem and solution. After previewing the book cover of *Imogene's Antlers* (Small, 1985), the students predicted the problem they thought the main character would face in the story, and we listed these responses on the board. Then, as I read the story, the students updated their predictions and suggested possible solutions. After we finished the story, the students discussed the actual problem and solution and compared them to their predictions. The students accurately predicted several of the problems and even came up with other potential problems. For example, Brianna suggested that the students would make fun of Imogene at school, and Taylor thought that birds would land on Imogene's antlers. None of the students predicted the surprise ending. They expected to see Imogene with the antlers still on head or possibly no antlers at all. Instead, they saw a picture of Imogene the following morning with no antlers, but sporting a full, beautiful tail of peacock feathers. Then, we discussed how having students predict what they thought would happen next while they read a story helped them understand, remember, and enjoy what they were reading.

Next, the students read *Ben's Teddy Bear* (Randell, 1996a). After the preview, each child drew a picture illustrating what he or she thought Ben's problem would be. Then, they read three pages and drew pictures depicting a possible solution. When they finished reading the story, each child drew a picture of the actual problem and solution. The students then took turns sharing and discussing their pictures. Because all the students demonstrated a need for practice identifying the problem and solution in a story, this became a skill that we addressed throughout the year.

The subsequent lessons focused on sequencing events. After we read *The Bear Who Wouldn't Share* (Mayer, 1987a), each student was given 13 slips of paper, each one identifying an event from the story. We began our work by categorizing the events as occurring at the beginning, in the middle, or at the end of the story. Next, we ordered the events in the beginning pile, then in the middle pile, and finally in the ending pile. Students took turns retelling the story using the ordered slips. Rick had no problem with sequencing, Taylor needed some help, and Clark and Brianna needed the most help and follow-up.

Because of the difficulties Brianna, Clark, and Taylor encountered while attempting to complete the sequencing project, I reshuffled the slips and allowed the students to use the book as they categorized the events into the beginning, middle, and end piles. Then we used logic and common sense to order each category of slips sequentially. I modeled some of the thinking necessary to complete the task as I reordered some of the slips, and the students began to mimic this thinking process after a few demonstrations.

Carolyn: Hmmm. I think Bear gathered his food before he went to sleep. He couldn't go out and get his food when he was already asleep. I think the first visitor arrived after winter arrived and it was cold and snowy. Otherwise, the visitor would not have been cold and hungry.

Rick: Bear had his dream before he shared his food. That's because his conscience said he was being selfish first.

Brianna: Yeah, and he didn't read the letters until springtime because that was when he woke up.

I noted improvement in all the students' abilities to sequence the events from a story. We continued to practice sequencing in their one-to-one sessions and during a couple more group lessons.

During our nine-week testing in December, Rick and Clark scored admirably and, according to their classroom teacher, were keeping up with most of their peers in the second-grade classroom. For these reasons, they proudly exited the program. To Brianna's delight, both of the new LEAP students were girls.

Our next two lessons focused on recalling information. These lessons were preceded by a lot of sight-word work with the question words *who*, *what*, *when*, *where*, *why*, and *how*. The students practiced recalling the details of a story using the teacher-made board game Question, Question (see Figure 15).

During another focus lesson, students played Question, Question using the story *There's an Alligator Under My Bed* (Mayer, 1987b). To play, each student chose a number between one and six. I rolled the die, and the student with the corresponding number began the game. "I'm first!" crowed Brianna. "I bet I'm gonna win this game!" She then rolled the die and moved her player four spaces along the board, where she landed on the "where" space. "Where did the boy think the alligator was hiding?" I asked. "Under the bed. That's easy!" Brianna responded. Clark, who was sitting to the left of Brianna, went next. He rolled a six and landed

---

Figure 15
Question, Question

After reading a story with the group, set up a board game by filling in the game squares with question words such as *who*, *what*, *when*, *where*, *why*, and *how*. A player rolls the die and moves one space for an odd number or two spaces for an even number. The teacher then asks the player a question about the story that begins with the word the student landed on. For example, if the student lands on the word *who*, the teacher might ask, "Who was the main character?" or "Who went into the bears' house while they were away on their picnic?"

You can add a twist to the game by dividing the game board into two halves. Decorate the first half with underwater animal stickers and the second half with jungle animal stickers. You compose and ask questions of students still on the underwater side. Once a player crosses the bridge and enters the jungle, however, the player to his or her right composes and asks the questions. If a player cannot answer a question, he or she loses a turn. The game continues until a player crosses the finish line.

---

on the "how" space. "How did the boy get to his bed without being eaten?" I asked. "I know that one!" chimed Rick. "Shhhh!" Clark said, "It's my turn." "Remember the rules," I reminded the students. "If you give an answer out of turn, you lose your turn." Then Clark said, "He had a board to his bed." "Right!" I said. We continued the game with the students answering my questions about the story until Brianna—as predicted—won.

We played the same game during another focus lesson using the book *Clifford's Good Deeds* (Bridwell, 1985). These lessons not only provided students with great practice reading the six question words and recalling details but also turned out to be the group's choice for favorite activity. As evidenced by these examples, games can serve a valuable purpose in the classroom such as generating meaningful conversation.

The next focus lesson covered the strategy of using context clues. First, we discussed and I modeled the use of context clues for figuring out unknown words and their meanings. Next, the students practiced using clues in the text to figure out the missing words first in sentences and then in paragraphs. As the students took turns reading a text that I had prepared by covering particular words with correction tape, they guessed these covered words. They identified the clues that helped them determine each word. Verbalizing their thinking was by far the hardest part of this task for the students but the most helpful. Verbalizing helped each child recognize the thinking process he or she was already using intermittently. Thus, students were more apt to apply the process, which in turn strengthened their adeptness at using it. My hope was that as they continued to apply context clues more often to their reading, they would internalize the process and improve their fluency and comprehension skills.

During our last focus lesson, the group worked on the same concept of using context clues. The students played the commercially prepared board game A Rare Fish by Frank Schaffer Publications. The first player picked a card containing a sentence that was missing one word and that offered three choices of words to fill in the blank. The player then read the sentence, determined the meaning of the missing word, matched the meaning to one of the choices, and explained the reasoning behind the choice.

For example, one card read, "The boy rode his _____ to school." The student determined that the missing word would be some type of transportation because of the word *rode* and that a child would be able to use it because it said the boy rode it. The choices were *sand*, *bike*, and *toy*. The student eliminated *sand* because it was not transportation. He eliminated *toy* because it didn't sound like something a child could ride to school. He determined the word *bike* fit the missing meaning because it is a means of transportation that most children have and ride.

After the first lesson, Mrs. Waffle and I supported the students' use of context clues whenever they were unable to figure out a particular word. For this reason, the second lesson on context clues reflected improvement in all the group members' abilities to use context clues and verbalize their reasoning.

The focus lessons were valuable for several reasons. Brianna, as well as each of the other group members, saw that she was not the only one having reading difficulties on certain concepts. The students learned a lot from listening to and conversing with each other during these lessons, and each had opportunities to shine in front of peers. The lessons provided different learning experiences and new knowledge that each student and I could refer back to as needed during other lessons. For example, I was able to say, "Brianna, remember in group when we learned to look at clues in the sentence? Maybe you could try that here," and "Brianna, you read this word during our game in group, remember? It was a question word."

The points of action were key aspects of the focus lessons. Each focus activity had a strong and clear purpose that was pertinent to the needs of our young readers and involved meaningful conversations with the teachers and one another. The classroom teacher and Mrs. Waffle and I repeatedly emphasized the purpose and use of the concepts. The students were consistently supported as they practiced applying the various ideas and strategies to their reading problems.

Brianna's Final Assessment Results

Brianna's final assessment results (May) were positive, but not as positive as we had hoped. In December, Brianna scored 94% on an oral reading analysis of a grade-level story she already had read with her class. In May, she scored a 99% on an oral reading analysis of a grade-level story she had never seen before but would read with her class within the next week. Her scores appeared good until I factored in Brianna's reading behaviors. Brianna was reading word by word. She lost her place several times and was constantly stopping, looking at the pictures, and changing the subject. These behaviors indicated to me that Brianna was experiencing difficulties with the text and that her confidence on this selection was waning.

In December, Brianna correctly read 17 of the 20 words on the Ohio Word Test. In March and May she correctly read 20 out of 20 words. In December, she accurately wrote 27 words from her own memory on the Writing Vocabulary Test. In March she wrote 46 words, and in May she wrote 35 words. On the Dictation Test, she scored 37 out of 37 in December and 36 out of 37 in March and May. But these three tests are normed for first-grade students.

Brianna scored 40% on comprehension questions in December, 56% in March, and 57% in May. Of course, the stories were at grade level and progressively more difficult, but there still was not a great deal of improvement. Brianna's reading level was below 1 in August (refer to Table 3 on page 94) and by May she was reading instructionally at level 13, which is still a first-grade level.

With summer break approaching, I worried that the progress Brianna had made could be lost if she didn't continue reading and applying the strategies and skills she had acquired over the year. I put together a booklist with suggested readings at levels appropriate for Brianna. I also sent home a packet of entertaining ideas Brianna and her family could do to help her engage with, think about, and expand on her readings. I wanted to keep Brianna writing, too, so I gave her fun writing ideas to respond to in a summer diary.

Reflection Point 4.10

Create a plan for one of your students to follow over the summer months. What suggestions could you make? What activities would be helpful? How could you support your student's transition to the next grade?

Follow-Up

When Brianna entered third grade, she was tested for learning disabilities. It was determined that she did not have a learning disability but was doing the best she could do. Luckily, our school was small enough to have room for a group from the third grade to attend LEAP lessons. So, Brianna's classroom teacher, Mrs. Waffle and I, and her family planned to work together again to help Brianna do the best she could do day by day for another school year.

Conclusion

We knew that Brianna had read about 140 LEAP books over the course of the year. We also knew that our meaningful conversations had helped improve her understanding of the reading process; that the element of choice had engaged her, made learning more fun, and provided her with a sense of ownership and control over her reading progress; she had received pertinent instruction; family and teachers had given her consistent support and encouragement; and she had a clearer picture of the purpose for reading and learning to read. Because of the LEAP program, Brianna was a better reader. But the reality was that Brianna was not reading at second-grade level and she was at the end of her second-grade year.

Why did I choose to write about Brianna when there were other students who progressed beautifully and who even exited LEAP in less than a year? I wrote about Brianna because she represents some of our most challenging learners. She was affected by several unhappy situations at a very young age. Coping with the emotional effects of these upheavals along with inconsistent school experiences had caused Brianna to internalize some ineffective strategies for learning. The challenge was not only to teach Brianna effective reading strategies but also to undo the ineffective ones.

By using the five points of action—meaningful conversation, choice, pertinent instruction, consistent support, and purpose—Brianna was able to make good progress and was on her way to becoming an enthusiastic, successful, and independent reader.

Chapter 5

Working Miracles in Your Classroom

*It's the last day of school and the students have just left the LEAP
classroom loaded with new books, packets full of summer reading
activities, a calendar of daily ideas, booklists, draft books, pencils,
bookmarks, and other treasures garnered during the school year. I,
Bev Wirt, return to my suddenly empty and quiet classroom feeling a
little empty myself. I think about all the lessons my students are
taking with them and hope they will not be forgotten during the
hiatus. I also think about the love of reading I saw in my classroom
and hope it won't fade. As I finish closing my room for the summer,
Ms. Peters, a first-grade teacher, comes in.*

> Ms. Peters: *I just stopped by to tell you again how amazed I am
> at the many little miracles that happened in the
> LEAP room this year. These students start the year
> knowing very little and come out as readers. I
> couldn't have done it alone.*

*I thank her and finish packing with a smile on my face, knowing
that I couldn't have done it alone either.*

All teachers want to work miracles in their classrooms. Like
Ms. Peters, you are probably working with more than one to
four students at a time. In this chapter, we suggest additional
ways to incorporate the five points of action in teaching small groups of
students or the whole class. Here are some ideas to bring meaningful
conversation, choice, pertinent instruction, consistent support, and
purpose to the classroom reading experience.

Meaningful Conversation

Meaningful conversations were a powerful factor in Allison's, Joshua's, and Brianna's growth during their year in LEAP. The one-to-one design enabled these conversations. We were able to add value to the routine chatter and meaning to discussion, elevating this talk to the level of meaningful conversations.

Teachers have many opportunities to develop these meaningful conversations in their daily lessons and routines. Small guided reading groups are one framework for reading instruction dependent on meaningful conversation. For example, in a guided reading group, the teacher might begin a meaningful conversation about a particular story the group has read by having the students compare and contrast the new text with a previously read text. The new text may lead the students to remember and share their own relevant personal experiences. This type of meaningful conversation teaches the students how to comprehend a text by linking the known to the unknown. Even though small groups lend themselves to more opportunities for participation and more personal choice of reading materials, meaningful conversation can still take place in a whole-class setting and be valuable to the students.

Besides improving comprehension, meaningful conversation also can support vocabulary development. Hearing new words or words used in new ways from peers and teachers during an exchange of ideas builds students' vocabularies. A small-group setting may provide a safer environment for some children to experiment with new vocabulary, but meaningful conversation within the whole-class setting is also important.

Not only does meaningful conversation develop comprehension and vocabulary, it also helps students expand their schema or knowledge base. As students listen to others speak from their own experiences and worldviews, their own world knowledge increases. For example, the book *Moms and Dads* (Randell et al., 1996c) refers to a veterinarian. Children who have never heard this word can learn about it by listening to classmates discussing their experiences with veterinarians.

By design, literature circles encourage meaningful conversation among peers about a commonly shared book (Daniels, 1994). In a literature circle, students assume roles such as discussion director, connector, summarizer, and vocabulary enricher. By taking on these roles, students learn how to effectively report information as well as share ideas. The difference between literature circles and guided reading groups is the leadership role. In a literature circle, the students are responsible for reading, setting up guidelines for discussions, and maintaining an atmosphere of acceptance and equality.

Paired reading arrangements provide another opportunity for students to converse with peers. Partners can read together with the goal of retelling periodically. After one child reads a few pages, the other child can provide a retelling. Then, they can reverse roles.

Reading conferences, or brief meetings between the teacher and individual students, offer the ultimate opportunity for meaningful conversations. Conferences should be scheduled to meet the needs of the teacher and the student. As the teacher guides the conversation, he or she gains understanding to plan pertinent instruction. The child benefits from being able to freely express opinions and ideas without competition or fear of criticism. The exchange of ideas enhances the student–teacher bond, motivates students, supports their vocabulary growth, expands their knowledge base, and increases their comprehension. Classroom teachers need to be determined and dedicated to make reading conferences a part of their classroom routine. It's not easy to find the time, but, from our own experiences and those of other teachers, we know that the conversation generated in this type of encounter is invaluable.

Meaningful conversation also can take place with volunteers or parents. Sentence starters, open-ended questions, and suggested discussion topics guide these opportunities. For example, discussions between students and parents could center on how their actions might differ if they had been a character in the book.

There are many opportunities for meaningful conversation with your students because there is no specific time or topic requirement. Meaningful conversation simply needs to be sincere and authentic to yield great rewards.

*Reflection Point 5.1*_____

In what ways do you stimulate meaningful conversations in your classroom? Name and discuss at least three things a teacher should avoid if he or she hopes to promote meaningful conversation.

_____

Choice

Allison's, Joshua's, and Brianna's learning was enriched by the choices they were invited to make. We frequently offered our students choice of materials, the sequence of activities, and practice formats. These opportunities for choice gave them a feeling of control while effectively engaging them in the achievement of personal goals.

How is it possible to offer choices to a larger group? Book selection is an obvious opportunity for student choice. Ideally, every teacher has hundreds of books in the classroom divided into boxes according to reading levels so that the students can choose books at their appropriate levels. Other opportunities to acquire books include the following:

- book club offers
- birthday book donations
- yard sales
- grants
- donations from local businesses
- book collections from public libraries
- school libraries
- student-made books

Baskets of books on the same subject at various levels can offer students choice as they work on particular topics and themed activities. Bags of several appropriately leveled books can be stored at each student's desk to allow for choice during self-selected reading times. Crates of leveled books also allow students to choose reading material. Previously read books also can be displayed for rereading.

Offer children other opportunities for choice. Students can choose topics to read about and summarize for the rest of the class either in groups or individually. They can choose between summarizing, illustrating, creating a poem or song, or doing another activity when responding to a particular reading. Students might simply choose a location for independent reading. At times, children may choose their own reading partners. Remember, something as simple as letting the child pick the color of a marker to use offers choice. Anything that offers a student choice also offers him or her more control, results in greater involvement, and makes the activity more intriguing.

Reflection Point 5.2

Evaluate your classroom procedures and score yourself between 1–10 with 1 being no teacher control and 10 being total teacher control. Then, decide if more or less control would improve your students' ability to learn to read. List and discuss ways you can offer more choices to your students. If, however, you find you offer too many choices, which could you eliminate? Is it possible that allowing students more choices will give you greater control in your classroom?

Pertinent Instruction

Offering pertinent instruction is a crucial and challenging point of action for the classroom teacher. Students disengage when lessons are too difficult, too easy, or irrelevant to their lives. If we are to hold their attention for the maximum amount of time, we must be sure to know what they know and what they need.

Can the same instruction be pertinent for 27 young learners? We think so. When introducing new concepts, the whole-class setting may provide for the most pertinent instruction. For example, the teacher should model reading strategies to everyone the first time. The teacher may demonstrate the use of context clues for figuring out the meaning of unknown words. Together, students can highlight the little words in big words.

Another time whole-class instruction is pertinent is when the teacher wants to develop a common base of knowledge to support a theme. Suppose a teacher is beginning a unit on mammals. The teacher may need all the students to understand the characteristics that define a mammal. Then, the students can read books on mammals at their own levels to reinforce the teacher's presentation and to find more information to share with the class. Or, the class story of the week might involve some unfamiliar ethnic traditions. The teacher can acquaint the class with specific information that builds a foundation for understanding the story.

When presenting a significant and challenging piece of text, a whole-class format may be most efficient. In most classrooms the basal readers or anthologies and the science, social studies, and math textbooks are above the reading level of a good number of the students. Whole-class instruction will develop specialized vocabulary, support comprehension, and make the attainment of certain goals possible for all students. Often content area textbooks for first grade, for example, have the same number of words per page, sentence complexity, content-related vocabulary, and text features at the beginning of the year as at the end. Whole-class presentations discussing graphs, maps, and text features as well as clarifying vocabulary are necessary for these materials to be meaningful to students.

Reflection Point 5.3

Select three students, one high performing, one average, and one struggling. Ask each student to read the same section of a school- or district-adopted text. Have each child retell this section. Take note of the differences and use them to identify pertinent teaching points that would have made the student more successful.

At times, a teacher may choose to group his or her students to make pertinent instruction more specific to students' individual needs. For example, a minilesson on identifying settings in stories might result from analysis of retelling assessments. Only the students with a need for such a lesson would participate in this group. Guided reading groups may focus on reading practice at appropriate levels. With good classroom management, teachers can even provide one-to-one tutoring when necessary.

Pertinent instruction must be balanced between small-group and whole-group instruction. The needs of the students dictate the balance. Whole-group instruction can be pertinent if the goal is well thought out and the methods align with the goal.

Consistent Support

Consistent support requires that teachers, parents, and student or community volunteers share a similar philosophy about reading and about learners. The classroom teacher must be cognizant of his or her own reading philosophies and be sure everyone else working with students understands them and works together accordingly. For example, a teacher who believes that all children can learn will share this philosophy with students, parents, other teachers, and volunteers. And a teacher who believes it is important for each student to read at home every night will communicate this belief to the student's family. A student working to use strategies to decode challenging words will develop these skills more quickly if consistently encouraged to use these strategies at school and at home.

Reflection Point 5.4

Take some time to think about your own personal teaching philosophy. Compose a brief philosophy statement. Consider displaying this statement in your classroom and sharing it with parents, administrators, volunteers, and students.

There are many ways a teacher can communicate with other teachers, students, and their families. A teacher should choose from the following options those that are compatible with his or her own schedule and personality:

website	home visits
e-mail	weekly reading tips
newsletters	classroom visits
weekly reports	conferences
individual notes	letters
parent nights	meetings
phone calls	

Consistent support means that everyone who is involved in the student's education must be an advocate for the learner. This attitude creates a safe atmosphere for risk taking that is necessary if students are to learn and grow. We've all seen students who have been given mixed messages about the importance of reading and their own abilities. These children, at best, are confused and, at worst, just don't care. Part of every teacher's job description is, or should be, setting up and maintaining lines of clear communication so that this necessary support exists and is consistent.

Purpose

Achieving a purpose can be compared to playing a board game. The end is clear to all players, and all the little squares on the board lead toward that end. Classrooms have many purposes or goals to accomplish each day. It is sometimes easy during the whirlwind of a busy day for the teacher and the students to lose sight of the end purpose. For this reason all short-term goals and activities, the little squares on the game board, should be planned and presented with the end purpose in mind. If they don't lead to the end purpose, they don't belong in the game.

Often, teachers think that the product is the purpose of the lesson. We think the process is the true purpose and where the value lies. For example, writing a sentence to summarize a level 7 book produces a product. However, the actual purpose of writing a sentence to summarize a level 7 book involves reading, internalizing information, inferencing, and drawing conclusions—all processes essential to literacy success and the true purpose of the lesson.

When a teacher designs lessons, it should be with the true purpose in mind and the end in sight, rather than to simply occupy students' time. He or she must clearly communicate the purpose to the students as well. For example, when a teacher wants to have a small-group guided reading lesson, he or she must plan meaningful activities to engage the other students in authentic reading and share the justification with them.

Merely completing an activity may not move a child toward the purpose. Students need to be cognizant of what they are doing and why they are doing it. The teacher needs to provide students with this information.

Reflection Point 5.5

Choose a particular purpose and, with that purpose in mind, develop a few independent or small-group activities. Be sure to include an explanation of the purpose for the students.

Conclusion

The three of us—Bev, Carolyn, and Kathleen—met at a favorite restaurant to decide on terminology for the findings of our yearlong experiences with Allison, Joshua, and Brianna.

Carolyn: How about calling them *impellers* since they moved our students forward in their reading in a powerful way?

Kathleen: I don't know. That makes me think of old airplane propellers or boat motors.

Bev: I picture someone being impaled to a tree by a spear!

The five points of action, as we finally called them, are the message of this book. Meaningful conversation, choice, pertinent instruction, consistent support, and purpose prove to be necessary components of a successful reading program. This is true in classrooms as well as in support programs.

We expect that you may have realized that you already apply many or all of the five points of action to your instruction. If so, we encourage you to use these points in ways that support the needs of the individual students in your classroom. We hope that you experience many miracles in your classroom as you help your students become successful and eager readers.

References

Allington, R.L. (2001). *What really matters for struggling readers: Designing research-based programs*. New York: Longman.

Allington, R.L. (2002). What I've learned about effective classroom teaching from a decade of studying exemplary elementary classroom teachers. *Phi Delta Kappan, 83*(10), 740–747.

Clay, M.M. (1988). *Reading recovery: A guidebook for teachers in training*. Portsmouth, NH: Heinemann.

Clay, M.M. (1993). *An observation survey of early literacy achievement*. Portsmouth, NH: Heinemann.

Costa, A.L. (1987). *The school as a home for the mind*. Arlington Heights, IL: Skylight.

Cunningham, P.M., & Allington, R.L. (1999). *Classrooms that work: They can all read and write*. New York: Longman.

Daniels, H. (1994). *Literature circles: Voice and choice in the student-centered classroom*. York, ME: Stenhouse.

Dombey, H. (1999). Reading! What children need to learn and how teachers can help them. *Reading Online*. Retrieved July 30, 2004, from http://www.readingonline.org/international/Dombey.html

Fountas, I.C., & Pinnell, G.S. (1996). *Guided reading: Good first teaching for all children*. Portsmouth, NH: Heinemann.

Gambrell, L.B. (1996). Creating classroom cultures that foster reading motivation. *The Reading Teacher, 50*, 14–25.

Good, T.L., & Brophy, J.E. (1999). *Looking in classrooms* (8th ed.). Boston: Allyn & Bacon.

Harvey, S., & Goudvis, A. (2000). *Strategies that work: Teaching comprehension to enhance understanding*. Portland, ME: Stenhouse.

Johns, J.L. (2001). *Basic reading inventory* (8th ed.). Dubuque, IA: Kendall/Hunt.

Johns, J.L., & Lenski, S.D. (1997). *Improving reading: A handbook of strategies*. Dubuque, IA: Kendall/Hunt.

Keene, E.O., & Zimmermann, S. (1997). *Mosaic of thought: Teaching comprehension in a reader's workshop*. Portsmouth, NH: Heinemann.

Miller, D. (2002). *Reading with meaning: Teaching comprehension in the primary grades*. Portland, ME: Stenhouse.

Routman, R. (2003). *Reading essentials: The specifics you need to teach reading well*. Portsmouth, NH: Heinemann.

Shearer, A.S., & Homan, S.P. (1994). *Linking reading assessment to instruction: An application worktext for elementary classroom teachers*. New York: St. Martin's.

Taberski, S. (2000). *On solid ground: Strategies for teaching reading K–3*. Portsmouth, NH: Heinemann.

Children's Literature References

Barton, B. (1993). *The little red hen*. Ill. K. Brown-Wing. New York: HarperCollins.

Bernard, R. (1996). *What Seahorse saw*. Boston: Houghton Mifflin.

Bridwell, N. (1985). *Clifford's good deeds*. New York: Scholastic.

Burnett, F.H. (1911). *The secret garden*. New York. HarperCollins.

Butler, A. (1989). *Teeny tiny Tina*. Ill. K. van Gendt. Scarborough, ON: Prentice Hall Ginn.

Child, A. (1992). *Charlie the dinosaur*. New York: Simon & Schuster.

Cowley, J. (1994). *Good for you*. Ill. E. Fuller. Bothell, WA: Wright Group.

Cowley, J. (1996a). *The long, long tail*. Ill. M. Beaslley. Bothell, WA: Wright Group.

Cowley, J. (1996b). *Mr. Grump*. Ill. W. Hodder. Bothell, WA: Wright Group.

Cowley, J. (1996c). *The tiny woman's coat*. Ill. E. Fuller. Bothell, WA: Wright Group.

Cowley, J. (1996d). *Where are you going, Aja Rose?* Ill. R. Murphy. Bothell, WA: Wright Group.

Curtis, J.L. (1995). *When I was little: A four-year-old's memoir of her youth*. Ill. L. Conell. New York: HarperTrophy.

Cushman, S. (1990). *Fuzz and the buzz*. Ill. P. Briles. Carson, CA: Educational Insights.

Cutting, J. (1996). *Run*. Ill. J. van der Voo. Bothell, WA: Wright Group.

Dee, A., & Scott, A. (1993). *Brittany the brontosaurus*. Ill. W. Bird. New York: Simon & Schuster.

Everitt, B. (1992). *Mean soup*. New York: Trumpet Club.

Feely, J. (1999a). *The giant gingerbread man*. Littleton, MA: Sundance.

Feely, J. (1999b). *Tarantula*. Littleton, MA: Sundance.

Giles, J. (1996). *My accident*. Ill. P. Cutter. Crystal Lake, IL: Rigby.

Haber, A. (1996). *Grasshopper and ant*. Ill. N. Spier. Boston: Houghton Mifflin.

Horn, N. (1998). *Good morning*. New York: McGraw-Hill.

Kahn, P. (1996). *I like cats*. Ill. J. Westerman. Boston: Houghton Mifflin.

Lang, G. (1999). *Socks off!* Littleton, MA: Sundance.

London, J. (1996). *Froggy goes to school*. Ill. F. Remkiewicz. New York: Puffin.

Marzollo, J. (1991). *In 1492*. Ill. S. Bjorkman. New York: Scholastic.

Mayer, M. (1987a). The bear who wouldn't share. In *Little Critter's bedtime storybook* (pp. 22–29). Racine, WI: Western.

Mayer, M. (1987b). *There's an alligator under my bed*. New York: Dial.

McLean, A. (1993). *The bus ride*. Glenview, IL: Scott Foresman.

Medearis, A.S. (1994). *Harry's house*. Ill. S. Keeter. New York: Scholastic.

Prince, S. (1999). *Mr. Wolf tries again*. Ill. P. Bajer. Littleton, MA: Sundance.

Randell, B. (1994). *Baby bear's present*. Ill. I. Lowe. Crystal Lake, IL: Rigby.

Randell, B. (1996a). *Ben's teddy bear*. Ill. G. Rees. Crystal Lake, IL: Rigby.

Randell, B. (1996b). *Blackberries*. Ill. I. Lowe. Crystal Lake, IL: Rigby.

Randell, B. (1996c). *Cat and Mouse*. Ill. I. Lowe. Crystal Lake, IL: Rigby.

Randell, B. (1996d). *Hermit Crab*. Ill. J. Bruere. Crystal Lake, IL: Rigby.

Randell, B. (1996e). *Kitty and the birds*. Ill. B. Greehatch. Crystal Lake, IL: Rigby.

Randell, B. (1996f). *Lucky goes to dog school*. Ill. W. Crosset. Crystal Lake, IL: Rigby.

Randell, B. (1996g). *The merry go round*. Ill. E. Lacey. Crystal Lake, IL: Rigby.

Randell, B. (1996h). *Stop!* Ill. M. Thomas. Crystal Lake, IL: Rigby.

Randell, B., Giles, J., & Smith, A. (1996a). *Dads*. Photo. J. Ussher. Crystal Lake, IL: Rigby.

Randell, B., Giles, J., & Smith, A. (1996b). *Dressing up*. Photo. C. Parker. Crystal Lake, IL: Rigby.

Randell, B., Giles, J., & Smith, A. (1996c). *Moms and dads*. Crystal Lake, IL: Rigby.

Rap, L., & Young, K.E. (1991). *Sherman's book of nursery rhymes* (pp. 25–27). New York: Simon & Schuster.

Saltis, N. (1999). *Snake's dinner*. Ill. M. Gardner. Littleton, MA: Sundance.

Schmidt, K. (1967). *The gingerbread man*. New York: Scholastic.

Small, D. (1985). *Imogene's antlers*. New York: Crown.

Wells, R. (1997). *Read to your bunny*. New York: Scholastic.

Wood, L. (1997). *Bump, bump, bump*. New York: Oxford.

Zane, R.M. (1998). *Vera's vegetables*. New York: McGraw-Hill.

Index

Note: Page references followed by *b* or *f* indicate boxes or figures, respectively.